HOMELIFE

Preparing Your Child For Success at School

HOMELIFE

Preparing Your Child For Success at School

by

CHERI FULLER

HONOR

A Division of Harrison House, Inc.
Tulsa, Oklahoma

Unless otherwise indicated,
all Scripture quotations are taken from
the *King James Version* of the Bible.

Cover photograph by Scott Miller.

*HOMELIFE — Preparing Your Child
for Success at School*
ISBN 0-89274-511-8
Copyright © 1988 by Cheri Fuller
P. O. Box 72
Yarmouth, Maine 04096

Published by Honor Books
A Division of Harrison House, Inc.
P. O. Box 35035
Tulsa, Oklahoma 74153

DEDICATION

To
my children,
Justin, Chris and Alison,
who light up my life,

and, especially,
my husband, Holmes,
my best and dearest encourager.

CONTENTS

ACKNOWLEDGMENTS

Special thanks to Rhana Robison for her contribution to "Re-establishing Stability" in Chapter 4. My thanks to Dr. Margaret Loeffler, Dr. Charles and Sue Gouaux, Dr. Lauren Bradway, Karen Gale, Sally Conway, Dr. Dale Jordan, Dr. Diana Waters and Dr. Eugene Walker for their input and suggestions.

My thanks also to a special group of teachers and mothers who shared their experiences and suggestions: Patti Milburn, Lynn Fuller, Carole Ashmore, Shirley Pugh, Jerry Gautreaux, Kay Bishop, Marilyn Morgan, Melanie Hemry, Joanna Smith, Corrie Sargeant, Cynthia Morris, Joyce Findley, Vicki Hamilton, Dana Smith, Vivian Nida, Freeda Richardson, Diana Purser, and Candy Snowbarger. And to Kathryn Fanning and her writing class, thanks for encouragement in the early stages of this project.

Chapter 1

EXCELLENCE:
WHERE DOES IT BEGIN?

Recently my son asked me, as we walked around the block, "Mom, why aren't you writing something exciting like Stephen King does? Why have you been working so long on that book about kids' education?"

As I gathered my thoughts, I remembered back to 1969 when I began teaching English and history at North Junior High School in Waco, Texas. Then I recalled the different schools I had taught in since then: high school, elementary school and the freshman level in college. I thought about how, during those years, I had seen students' skills — in reading, composition, history and math — slide steadily downhill. I didn't have to read the newspaper to know that educationally we were a nation at risk.

Corporate leaders were charging that most youngsters leave school lacking the discipline, work habits and command of the English language necessary to hold a job, thus dooming themselves to failure in life. Teachers were reporting a tragic loss of the American dream, that many children had lost the ability to see the value of English, algebra, and history. There was overcrowding and a lack of funding in many schools. Illiteracy rates were climbing, SAT scores were falling, and American students were scoring poorly on achievement tests in comparison with students from other countries. And many of the youngsters I saw didn't have the reading ability or study habits to excel or even survive in high school, much less out in the adult world.

"I know Donnie is failing, but I feel powerless to change the situation," the mother of an eighth-grade student told me one afternoon. "What can I do?"

At teacher conferences other parents just like her shared with me that they wanted to improve their children's education, but felt inadequate and helpless.

Researchers say that most parents want to be involved in their children's schoolwork, but do not know what to do or where to start. That's why I wrote this book. For, through those years of teaching, I began to realize that we parents are the ones who really need the encouragement and help. Why? *Because, whether they are in public, private or a home school, we are our children's best teacher, more important to their education than anyone else in the world! And second, because the key to our children's lifelong learning and success in school lies in the quality of their homelife, not only during the important first five years of their life, but throughout their entire school experience.*

In this book I will share with you some simple tools to help you develop a home environment that is rich in learning resources for an excellent education for your child. I will share with you:

- How to develop a stable homelife supportive of learning

- How to understand your child's learning style and maximize his study

- How to discover your child's intelligence gifts and

talents and how to develop them for higher self-esteem and motivation

- How to help your child become a lifelong writer and reader

- How to teach your youngster some vital study strategies that will multiply his retention and raise his grades

- How to communicate with school personnel, solve problems that arise and engage in an effective conference with a teacher

- How to keep your child learning during the summer

With the current explosion of technology in which a microcomputer can become obsolete almost before it gets to the retail market, we cannot teach our young people all the facts and formulas they will need to know to succeed in life. But if we can help them to develop motivation and initiative, to learn to think critically, to read well, and to communicate effectively in speech and writing, then they will continue to learn long after their formal education has ended.

You may be asking questions like: How long are these activities going to take? How do you expect me to make time for these educational concerns in my already overcrowded schedule? How will I find the time? These are valid questions. Besides being a parent at home with a hectic schedule of caring for a family, you may be a member of a two-career family, juggling the demands of a job with the added responsibilities of a household and child rearing. You may be a single parent, dealing with the terrific time-pressures that go with trying to handle job stress, financial distress, and parenting problems — all by yourself.

In this book I will give you some ideas for your child's learning, whether he attends a public, private or home school. These ideas can be incorporated into your lifestyle, whether you are a working mother or an in-the-home parent. They are suggestions for things you can include in the time you do have to spend with your child, without causing you to become a taskmaster or requiring you to hold a two-hour study hall every night. I will show you ways to be a positive role model for learning; how to be a facilitator, and an encourager.

You will see that the time you do spend with your child in a learning activity, however simple or complicated it may be, will be multiplied back to you, as your child grows to become a more independent student during his junior high school years. Whether it is reading aloud, drilling for a Spanish test, discussing a newspaper article around the dinner table, or having your child keep a journal on travels, you will be building a foundation for him to become a lifelong learner and a success in school.

If you will follow my suggestions, you will learn how to provide a home environment in which resources are available to help your child become creative and to develop good study habits and a sense of curiosity. You will talk about counting as you are at the grocery store. You will learn to leave your child notes in his lunchbox saying, "I love you; have a good day," or ones on his desk that say, "Clean up your room," or "Keep up the good work." You will learn to give your child *role models, resources, reasons* (and encouragement) to read, write, use math skills, and explore the world around him. In return, he will discover the joy of learning, and thus lay a firm foundation for success in school.

These and other keys to school success are what this book is all about: inside information I have accumulated from being an educator and also the mother of three children who are not perfect students and who need study strategies and encouragement too.

Let's keep academics in proper perspective. We need to maintain a balance between school work and other areas important to the growth of our children: emotionally, intellectually, physically and spiritually, as well. Relational growth is also vital to our children's life and learning.

"A family is a formation center for human relationship," writes Edith Shaeffer in *What Is a Family?* "The family is the place where the deep understanding that people are significant, important, worthwhile, with a purpose in life, should be learned at an early age. The family is the place where children should learn that human beings have been made in the image of God and are therefore very special in the universe."[1]

Your child's relationship with you is central to his education. Dr. Margie Golick, speaking about what children need to know to become successful learners in school, says: "Many of the pleasures of learning and living come from relationships with other people. A child will be receptive to the teacher's teaching only if he has learned to care about the adults in his world. This kind of caring grows out of his own experiences of being cared about and respected and enjoyed."[2]

New studies show that *throughout school years*, more than any other factor, *it is what the parents do at home* that makes the difference between success or failure for children. Even after they reach school age, children spend an average of only 13 percent of their time in school. The other 87 percent of their time is spent at home or under parental influence and direction.

From the beginning, by example perhaps more than by word, parents teach attitudes, values, and habits that help shape their children's character, now and throughout life. Children learn what they live. As Henry Ward Beecher said, "What the mother sings to the cradle goes all the way down to the coffin."[3]

Psychologist Dr. Charles Gouaux of Gouaux Clinical Associates, St. Louis, Missouri, has said that one of the most powerful things a parent can do to enhance, strengthen and support his child's education is to let the child see him enjoying his own curiosity, using and expanding his intellect, and learning from new experiences. As *you love learning*, your child learns to enjoy his own curiosity, intellect, creativity and talent. He becomes, in fact, a lifelong learner.

As a parent, it is a privilege to watch God's purpose unfold in a child's life. And a part of that plan involves the child's education — because that is preparation for the life and work he will pursue. Becoming literate and mastering certain language, math and study skills, learning the history of our nation and world, learning to organize his time, to be responsible, to apply himself to a task — all these are part of the educational process.

But most important, we want our children to become *lifelong learners* who will seek out and pursue knowledge in their own chosen field of interest and talent.

In addition to academics, there are the life skills that young people need to develop — how to cook, listen, forgive, save money, solve problems, do laundry, and many other practical skills that will help them become independent.

There are opportunities to share with our children the heritage of what we know — however simple that may be. It may be to plant a garden, to do woodworking or calligraphy, to cross-stitch, to properly wash and wax a car, or to play tennis. These skills are gifts of love imparted from one generation to the next. They bring esteem and confidence as the child learns to do them well. And a special relationship develops that goes beyond the activity of learning how to sail a boat or knit or play the guitar. There are moments of closeness as you share your skill or knowledge with your child.

Recently I heard a mother say: "I'm not a teacher. I didn't even like school myself, so I don't have much to teach my children." You may feel that same way, but I want to encourage you that you have much to teach your child. Let me give you an example from my own everyday life.

Early this evening, my daughter, Alison, and I were riding bikes together. Alison was riding ahead of me on her new ten-speed bicycle. As we went around the curves and onto a busy residential street, I coached her a little from behind. A car zoomed up behind me. "Stay a little closer to the right curb," I called out to her. "Better stop at the corner and look both ways," I cautioned a little later. "Good job when you signaled to turn left!" I encouraged.

Supervising a child's education is much like that bike ride. The educational system is like a maze or a busy city street. Most youngsters need some personal coaching and a lot of encouragement if they are to learn how to get through it all without calamity.

That is our job as parents. We can't ride the bike for our child, but we can coach him until he can maneuver through the busy street on his own and arrive safely at his destination. We can make sure that he has the right equipment for the trip. We can know where he's going. We can help him up when he falls. We can even help him get a tire fixed when it goes flat.

Similarly, as you come to know your child and his abilities, you will begin to understand that what you do is more important to his academic success than his IQ, your financial status, or any other factor. This book will equip you to help your child so that, in spite of the problems he may face in school, whether public or private, he will be prepared to learn, to get the most out of what the school offers, and to develop the skills needed to succeed.

As parents, our goal is to prepare our children for the great purpose God has for their lives, so let's get on with the job!

Footnotes

[1]Edith Shaeffer, *What Is a Family?* (Old Tappan: Fleming H. Revell Company, 1975), p. 69.

[2]Margie Golick, *Deal Me In: The Use of Playing Cards in Teaching and Learning* (New York: Monarch Press, Simon and Schuster, Inc., 1981), p. 4.

[3]Henry Ward Beecher, *Proverbs from Plymouth Pulpit,* quoted in the *International Thesaurus of Quotations,* p. 453.

Chapter 2

WHAT'S YOUR CHILD'S LEARNING STYLE?

Kate memorizes written material quickly and puts together complicated jigsaw puzzles with ease. But she can't remember her homework assignments unless she writes them down.

John has excellent coordination and shines as an athlete, but fidgets in the classroom and doesn't like to read.

Hillary has a large vocabulary and expresses herself well. However, she talks out of turn in class and can't follow directions unless they're explained orally.

Kate, John and Hillary aren't learning-disabled. They just have different learning styles, as we all do.

One night our daughter, Alison, had thirty irregular verb forms to memorize in the present, past and past-perfect tenses — that's ninety words to be tested on the next morning! She had been sick the day of the explanation and practice in class, so at first the task looked overwhelming.

I went over the list with her orally. Then I showed her how to make a tape recording of each verb and its forms (freeze, froze, frozen; draw, drew, drawn; etc.). She enjoyed making the tape and played it over several times, reciting along with it. I gave her oral practice, and then tested her, circling the verbs she missed. She studied those again, saying them out loud. The whole process took about thirty minutes.

The next morning, Alison used her tape to practice the verb forms at breakfast. That day at school, she scored 95 percent on her English test and received a great boost in confidence. Now she uses this study method herself in history, spelling and French. This is a good example of using an understanding of learning style to develop study habits that work for a child. And you can develop study strategies for your child, too.

Teachers across the country are using information on learning styles to help children in their classrooms, but as a parent, you are actually better equipped than a teacher — who has 20 or 30 students in each class — to discover this valuable information about your child. Notice how he tackles a problem. Listen for clues when his teacher talks about how he performs in class.

If you understand how your child learns, you can maximize his or her use of study time at home. As your child comes to understand how he learns best, he will become an active, *rather than a passive, learner who takes more responsibility for his own instruction.*

"The passive learner usually doesn't learn much and the hostile student rarely learns anything worthwhile," says Charles E. Finn, Jr., Assistant Secretary for Research and Improvement, in *What Works.*[1] So helping your child become an active learner increases his enthusiasm for learning and builds on his strengths. In addition, you can help to develop strategies to use when he has difficulty understanding a concept, has information to memorize or tests to study for. With this information, children who have never before experienced success in the classroom can find learning much more rewarding.

As a parent, your learning style is probably different from your child's, and this is often the source of conflict when you try to help him with his homework.

What Is Learning Style?

Learning style refers to the way a person best takes in, understands and remembers information. According to Dr. Rita Dunn of the Center for the Study of Learning and Teaching Styles, St. John's University, New York, there are twenty-one different factors that make up learning style: such as whether a child learns best alone, or in a study group with peers, or in a highly structured setting with an adult.

Some children learn best in a quiet room, others with background noise; some learn best in logical steps, while others see the whole picture at once. Some children need more structure than others. Some learn best in an open-ended learning environment.[2]

> All of these unique factors show how God created each child individually, for His purpose. Just as your child has a distinct temperament, physical characteristics and personality, he also has a particular way of learning.

Research at several top universities shows that one factor that plays an especially important role in learning is perceptual strength, the "sensory channel" through which children take in information. For example, the *visual* learner understands and remembers best what he sees with his eyes. The *auditory* learner needs to hear and

21

verbalize the new information to understand it. The *kinesthetic* learner needs to involve touch and movement in the processing of new concepts. He needs to use his muscles by writing down or acting out the new material — because he learns by doing.

While most of us use all three systems for learning, scientists have discovered that in each of us one channel is more finely tuned than the others and thus exerts more influence upon our learning.

Read the following descriptions and then take the learning-style quiz.

Meghan, the Auditory Learner

Meghan talked early and constantly, with a wide and colorful vocabulary. Her speech was clear and she sounded like a little adult, relating riddles and creative stories to her family. She liked to make up stories and to role play on the playground. She was always a very sociable child.

Although bright, Meghan has difficulty in math. She has had trouble mastering the math facts, which slows her down while doing arithmetic problems. She is also easily distracted in class. Like most auditory learners, Meghan moves her lips or whispers while trying to memorize. She participates well in class discussions. She excels in foreign language. She follows oral directions easily and is quick to answer the teacher's oral questions.

Meghan needs to verbalize information — she must hear it and say it in order to best learn it.

Brian, the Visual Learner

Brian relies more on seeing things and visualizing them. As a baby, he could be quieted by the sight of his mother's face or by the movement of his crib mobile. As a toddler, he learned his colors quickly and when traveling in the car, he looked attentively at passing billboards, noticing details about them that were missed by his parents. Brian loves to draw. He has a vivid imagination.

Like other visual learners, Brian often closes his eyes or looks at the ceiling when he is memorizing or recalling information he is tested on. When he has to listen for an extended period in class, he begins to doodle, squirm or daydream.

Brian shines in math, where he can easily picture math problems and compute their answers in his head.[3]

Josh, the Kinesthetic Learner

Josh was a wiggly baby, and all through his early years, he was in perpetual motion. His means of exploring was dismantling, pulling and handling. Josh has excellent coordination — whether building a Lego castle or hitting a baseball. At age four he delighted his family with his ability to ride a bicycle without training wheels. He has superb gymnastic ability and is the star of the soccer team.

Because of his squirming and his short attention span, Josh has not been the teacher's favorite. He has difficulty following directions. He uses his fingers to count off items or to write in the air when trying to remember something.

Learning to read has proved very frustrating for Josh and he finds all academic subjects hard.

The Learning-Style Quiz

Check only those statements that accurately describe your child's behavior. Then for each statement, find the corresponding number in the categories below, labeled *visual, auditory* and *kinesthetic,* and circle it. A large number of circles in one category indicates a strong leaning in that direction.

1. Your child is quiet; he rarely volunteers answers.

2. Your child loves to communicate; he talks a lot.

3. Your child relates to you more in body and action than in words.

4. Your child loves putting together difficult puzzles.

5. Your child is in perpetual motion; he rarely sits still.

6. Your child remembers jingles, poems and television commercials.

7. Looking neat and being color-coordinated are important to your child.

8. Your child tries to touch everything he sees.

9. Your child is especially observant of details.

10. Your child has a messy appearance and keeps an untidy room and cluttered desk.

11. Your child is easily distracted by background noises.

12. Your child has a vivid imagination.

13. Your child stomps or slams the door when angry.

14. In his spare time, your child would most of all like to watch television or a movie.

15. Your child is very verbal and can express his feelings.

16. In his spare time, your child enjoys listening to a radio, record player or tapes.

17. Even as he gets older, your child prefers to try things out by touching and feeling.

18. Even when most upset, your child holds in his feelings.

19. In his spare time, your child would prefer to be playing, jumping, running or wrestling.

20. Your child can assemble almost anything without help from printed or pictured instructions.

21. Your child sorts out problems by talking about them.

22. Your child naturally sounds out words and is a good speller.

23. It is hard to hold your child's attention, especially for reading.

24. Your child hears oral directions and follows them readily.

Visual
1, 4, 7, 9, 12, 14, 18, 20

Auditory
2, 6, 11, 15, 16, 21, 22, 24

Kinesthetic
3, 5, 8, 10, 13, 17, 19, 23

How to Enhance Your Child's Learning Style

The *auditory learner* needs clear verbal explanations when presented with new or difficult material. He may need help decoding written directions. He is distracted by background noise while studying, so will retain most when studying in a quiet room.

The auditory learner often lacks the visual memory he needs for success in the classroom. Play games to improve his visual recall. For example, on a tray place a variety of interesting objects. Allow him to study them for 30 to 45 seconds, then take the tray away and ask him to list as many objects as he can remember. The card game Concentration also improves visual memory.

Because the auditory learner works best when he hears new information, a tape recorder is his best ally for effective study. Equip your child with a tape recorder, a blank tape and a series of flash cards with his lessons written on them. Then have him read into the machine each new fact he wants to remember. Have him say, for example, "Two plus two equals..." but tell him to omit the answer. Then have him replay the tape and answer the questions as often as necessary to learn the correct answers. He can make fill-in-the-blank tapes for each subject; also, he can summarize lectures on tape and play them back for review.

When studying spelling at home, he should say the word aloud as he writes it several times. On trips encourage him to record his observations in a journal. Take him to plays and musicals, and give him opportunities in speech, drama or creative writing.

A good study process for the junior high or high school auditory student:

- Listen carefully, take notes and tape record class lectures, if possible

- Discuss information with someone; study with a friend; teach it to Mom/Dad or brother/sister

- Reinforce material learned by reading and making notes or flashcards to use orally

- At test time, replay tape of class lecture; study class notes in sections and be orally tested on questions; or make a fill-in-the-blank study tape.

The *visual learner* can be the most hooked on television, so limit his TV time. Provide plenty of books and magazines in the areas of his favorite interests. Encourage him to read. Once the visual learner gets started, he often enjoys reading more than any other child.

The visual learner has the edge in elementary school because reading is a visual activity. But he may have difficulty later on if he doesn't develop good listening and communication skills as well. Telling stories to your child is a good way to improve his listening skills, especially if you take time to talk about the story afterward.

One game to play to enhance listening skills is Add-a-Sentence. Choose a title such as "My Life on the Moon," and ask each player to add a sentence to advance the story. Play "I went on a picnic." To begin, say, "I went on a picnic and I took apples." The next player must repeat what the previous player has said, adding a new picnic ingredient which begins with the next letter of the alphabet (for example, bananas). The game continues until someone fails to repeat correctly all the items on the list.

The visual learner works best from a list of jobs, crossing each one off as it is done. In school, have him keep an *assignment notebook* daily so he can follow through.

The visual learner is very distracted by a disorderly study area. He works best at a neat, organized desk. He will enjoy working alone and taking responsibility for his own work.

A good study method for the junior high or high school visual learner:

- Do some reading the night before new material is presented in class; notice charts, maps or graphs

- Take notes or make an outline of new material

- Listen carefully to class lecture and take good notes either on index cards or in outline form

- Make flashcards:

  On one side: concept or word

  On other side: explanation or meaning

- Make and take a sample test; go over questions and answers orally

The *kinesthetic learner* needs a multisensory phonics reading program (which uses plastic or sandpaper alphabet letters) and multisensory math (with concrete objects which focus on touch in learning, like "Mathematics Their Way," an activity-centered early childhood program which makes use of experience with familiar materials such as tiles, buttons, jars and mirrors).

At home, one of the best learning tools would be a large chalkboard. When new spelling words are introduced, the kinesthetic learner can write them in large letters on his chalkboard and then erase the letters with two fingers. Or he can practice writing spelling words on large colorful sheets of construction paper using first a marker, then a ballpoint, and then a bright crayon. He can practice math facts, history facts and vocabulary the same way. Making his own flashcards for any subject is a valuable activity.

Since action is the key for the kinesthetic learner, acting out vocabulary words helps him remember them. Likewise, acting out a scene of a story he is going to be tested on is helpful. Before a test, have him teach *you* the material using his chalkboard.

The kinesthetic learner often lacks good listening skills, so use games and activities at home to improve his auditory memory and listening ability. Play an advanced version of "Simon Says" in which you give the child a series of actions to perform in order. Tell stories, and let him listen to taped books on a cassette player. Read aloud as a family to improve his listening and comprehension skills, and remember that books with plenty of action will appeal to him most.

A good study method for the junior high or high school kinesthetic learner:

- When reading, highlight with a yellow highlighter important facts, headings and key words

- Always listen carefully during class lectures or presentations and be sure to take good notes

- Whenever possible, *apply* new information to something concrete; use a real situation, or teach someone else what is being learned

- Play a game with the information to be learned

- Make up a sample test and take it; go over the questions and answers orally before the final test

Notice that there is some overlapping in these study strategies, because we all take in information through hearing, seeing and doing, but have one channel that is strongest. We use that strength for introduction of new material or for studying for tests, and use the other channels to reinforce our understanding of what we are learning.

Lastly, knowledge of learning style is not a panacea for all learning problems, but it is a good tool to help a child develop his own effective study habits. It also helps him use his own sensory strength when he is frustrated, has low test scores or experiences difficulty in retaining basic information he will need later on.

Educators are beginning to admit that much of what is termed "learning disabilities" is really a matter of unqiue learning styles. Psychometrists (those who measure psychological variables) report that some children referred to as "learning disabled" are simply kinesthetic learners who have not been helped to use other learning channels. Often when a teacher uses only visual or auditory methods, the kinesthetic learners in the class become behavior problems.

It has been discovered that when these children are instructed in all three learning pathways — allowed to hear, see and especially to do — they show amazing progress.

In a large class, only the brightest or most motivated students are going to be successful. However, if your child understands his own learning style and how to work with it, he will enjoy school more and be more motivated, which will increase his changes for happiness both in and out of school.

Come up with your own ideas to match homework and study to the learning style of your child. Appreciate all his efforts. Whenever possible in the learning process, help him to *hear, see and do*. As you come to understand how he learns, you can be more supportive and effective when he needs help. Instead of pushing, give encouragement and support.

With these secrets to school success, both you and your child will find joy in learning.

Footnotes

[1] *What Works: Research About Teaching and Learning,* United States Department of Education: William J. Bennett, Secretary, 1986, p. 4.

[2] Rita Dunn, "Learning Styles: Link Between Individual Differences and Effective Instruction" (*North Carolina Educational Leadership, 1986*), p. 3.

[3] The author is grateful to Dr. Lauren Bradway of United Methodist Counseling Services (located in Oklahoma City, Oklahoma) for her insights about the visual learner.

Chapter 3

YOUR CHILD:
FULL OF PROMISE

What Does "Gifted And Talented" Mean?

Recently, I attended a state conference for teachers and parents of gifted, creative and talented children. Workshops were offered on the subject of how to make home and school more stimulating for these youngsters. The nature of these workshops is indicated by their titles, such as "Great Books Program," "Arts for the Talented Child," and "Stimulating Creativity in Young Children."

In public schools in our city, the term "gifted, creative, and talented" (usually shortened in most school programs to "gifted and talented") is used to refer to a select group of students who score above the ninety to ninety-six percentile on achievement or intelligence tests. These students then meet throughout the school year with top teachers in what are called "Promise Classes," designed to nurture the gifts of these exceptional children.

Although most programs for gifted children in this country have as their primary criterion for admission a score of 130 or more on standard intelligence tests, there is much controversy about what the term *gifted* actually means. Researchers are pointing out the limits of standardized testing for discovering "giftedness." Ethnic groups charge that standardized IQ tests are culturally biased in favor of middle-class whites. In most schools in California, psychometrists are no longer allowed to use IQ tests to determine students' "giftedness." Research suggests that a child's interests are valuable indicators of his talents. They suggest that observing the child at play and work is a much better way of predicting his potential and identifying his natural abilities.

In one workshop, we were asked:

Does your child:

- Learn quickly?

- Show interest in many subjects?

- Enjoy creativity in dance, drama, rhythm or music?

- Commit intensely to one or two hobbies?

- Exhibit a well-developed sense of humor?

- Improvise with commonplace materials?

- Use expressive speech?

- Tire of repetitious assignments?

- Enjoy solving problems?

- Want to know the how and why of things?

- Think of original ideas?

- Express feelings/emotions well?

Having three or more of these characteristics, we were told, classified a child as gifted.

Although experts say that "giftedness" cannot be truly assessed until a child is three or four years old, some signs of exceptional talent in infancy are: marked alertness, a high level of activity, and early advancement through childhood developmental stages.

At the conference we were told that about three million young people have scored 130 or more on IQ tests, thus qualifying them to be labeled "gifted." One percent of American children scored in the range of 160 and up. These latter students are called "profoundly gifted." Together, these two groups are supposed to represent those youngsters in our nation who deserve the special designation of "students of promise."

Yet while reading the brochure given out at the conference, I began to ask myself, "But aren't *all* children full of promise and potential for talent in some area?" Yes, some do have more math-science or language aptitude (the main criteria for IQ tests). But the fact is, every child is creative in his own unique way. Made in the image of an enormously creative God, each child has been gifted in some area, no matter what his physical handicaps or limitations may appear to be.

> "Some of the factors inside children waiting for someone with faith to trigger their growth are inherent talent, creativity, and aptitude."
>
> Marti Garlett
> *Who Will Be My Teacher?*[1]

Heather, a little girl I know, had a blood clot in her brain at birth, causing the right side to be "dead," according to the doctors. Although they disagreed about some details of the diagnosis, the doctors predicted she would not be able to talk, walk or speak.

Now five years old, Heather has experienced slow development, has needed therapy and operations on her right hand

and foot. But she attends school on her appropriate grade level, is very verbal, and enjoys learning. And she has already shown phenomenal musical talent, including the gift of perfect pitch. She has the ability to remember lyrics and melodies she has heard only once. At only two years of age, she said, "Mama, I need some paper to write my song," and proceeded to dictate lyrics to her mother and sing a lovely melody.

Our Job as Parents: Discovering and Developing Our Children's Gifts

How can we encourage the gifts our children have? By being interested, aware and supportive, we unlock our children's creativity and "giftedness."

"We helped our daughters look for their talents and gifts by giving them a wide variety of experiences around our home and, as we could afford it, in the community and through other means," says Sally Conway of Christian Living Resources in Fullerton, California. "They very early developed an interest in animals, both because of the variety of pets we had and because of our observing animals in nature. We took a lot of camping trips and always had our eyes open for animals, insects, trees, flowers and so on. We always had a wide variety of visitors in our home since we were a pastor's family. We encouraged them to try various hobbies, belong to 4-H clubs with various activities, and to have friends of all ages, races, and backgrounds."

She adds that she and her husband did a lot of talking about their daughters' interests and tried to be flexible when the girls had ideas and goals they considered to be out of line. "Interestingly, we learned a lot from *them*," she states, "and they have helped widen our visions and courage to try new things."

Family projects are a great way for children to use their talents together, each one doing what he or she enjoys the most. In order to prepare a play to perform for friends and family, for instance, one child can make the props, one can write the script and act, and the other can produce the play, advertise it and recruit kids for parts.

We cannot depend on the school to identify our children's talents. So each of us should be looking to detect and bring out their special abilities.

An enriched home environment with experiences in language, music, art, math, science, and writing nurtures a child's gifts. Out of the wide variety of projects in which he is involved in the community and beyond, he will surely find at least one (and usually more) that will really spark his natural interest.

Every child needs to develop his own skills and talents, to build self-esteem, to guard against feelings of worthlessness and inferiority, and to channel his energies. As Dr. James Dobson says in his excellent book, *Hide or Seek*: "It is your job as a parent to help him find them. Perhaps he can establish his niche in music — many children do. Maybe he can develop his artistic talent or learn to write or cultivate mechanical skills or build model airplanes or raise rabbits for fun and profit."[2]

What is important is finding *something* your child is good at and encouraging and investing in that skill. Consider his abilities. Don't be afraid to introduce him to your own favorite hobbies and to share your talents with him.

Dr. Lauren A. Sosniak, a research coordinator for the Development of Talent Project at the University of Chicago, interviewed 120 extremely talented men and women and their parents to determine how these people had developed such demonstrated ability. The study revealed that the parents interviewed had been interested in something and had enjoyed sharing it with their children "...from as early as when their children were born. They weren't waiting to see if their children suddenly became interested in music or athletics or academics."[3]

Find a field your child enjoys and has potential in, and do all you can to help him learn the basics of it. Remember that helping a child learn skills and develop talents takes patient involvement, investment and support over a period of time, often years.

As Cliff Schimmels says: "You don't have to overinflate his ego, but give him support...Watch him play his athletic contest, even if he isn't the star. Make the *child* important, rather than his accomplishment. That is doubly true if your child happens to be extremely good. Don't let him forget that his achievement is a gift from God, and it is his willingness to use that gift which is to be celebrated, not his success with it."[4]

We also encourage our children's talents when we listen to their songs or plays, when we sit down at the piano and listen to them practice, when we pay attention to what they have made and show interest in their developing skills. Since children have a great motivation to please the people they love the most (their parents!), our interest goes a long way toward encouraging the development of our children's talents.

> "Studies of accomplished musicians, athletes and historical figures show that when they were children, they were competent, had good social and communication skills, and showed versatility as well as perseverance in practicing their skill over long periods. Most got along well with their peers and parents. They constantly nurtured their skills. And their efforts paid off."
>
> *What Works*[5]

Research shows that, even more than good genes or pushy parents, sensitive nurturing is the most important aspect in the development of young talent. There is a difference between pressuring and pushing a child, and encouraging his gifts to bloom.

Constant criticizing of his performance discourages any youngster from developing his innate abilities.

As Lori McNeil, professional tennis player, says: "It was always important to me that I'm still Lori to my parents, on or off the court. It means a lot that their love and affection are not based on my winning or losing. Sometimes parents treat you different, or show disappointment when your performance is down. It's important for the child to understand that, win or lose, his parents' attitude is the same, their love and support stands."

Maybe your son loves track and works diligently at it, but will never be a Bruce Jenner. Perhaps your daughter loves music and practices faithfully, but will never be a Beverly Sills. We need to remember that the process of doing, participating and enjoying is important even if our children never reach the top of a certain field. The benefits are enormous: self-confidence and self-esteem are built; he learns discipline which can carry over into other areas; she learns perseverance and develops a personal identity which will help her not to be as vulnerable to peer pressure.

Seven Gifts and How to Encourage Them

We know that IQ tests do not tell the complete story of a child's potential. Since it measures primarily logical-mathematical and linguistic intelligence, a standardized test cannot, for example, reveal John's perfect pitch, Kimberly's super coordination, or Joanna's intuitive understanding of people or her ability to work with them. Thus, no written test can give a totally accurate picture of a child's full capabilities or gifts.

Dr. Howard Gardner, a neurology professor at Boston University, through a study of normal and gifted youngsters, has identified seven areas of intelligence in children. In his book, *Frames of Mind: The Theory of Multiple Intelligences,*[6] Dr. Gardner challenges the traditional assumption that intelligence can be measured by paper-and-pencil tests such as the Stanford-Binet, the most widely used intelligence test. According to Dr. Gardner, parent observation is the best indicator of a child's intelligence.

37

He describes five other areas of gifting in addition to the linguistic and logical-mathematical: musical, spatial, bodily-kinesthetic, knowledge of self, and knowledge of others (called the personal intelligences).

A child may show promise in several areas, or his blend of intelligences may produce a special ability, unique to him. But Dr. Gardner feels that, if properly encouraged, almost every child develops strengths in at least *one* particular area of "giftedness."

If we understand and appreciate these gifts, and know how to encourage them, our children can be happier and have higher self-esteem. So consider the following areas of talent, discover your child's personal potential, and enjoy helping him develop.

The Linguistic Gift

Molly talked in sentences by the time she was eighteen months old, and at age three had an unusually large vocabulary. She sounded like a little adult. At eight years of age, she wrote poems for fun and gave them as gifts to her parents. Before she started school, she taught herself to read. Molly is a language-gifted child.

The child with high language intelligence is fascinated with words and enjoys puns, riddles and limericks. He can recite a story or a poem which has been read to him only a few times.

Since the verbally-oriented child loves to read, supply him with plenty of language resources and read to him every day. Read classics which are over his age level. Read poetry as a family. Encourage dramatization of his favorite stories.

He may enjoy writing and producing a play for the neighborhood. Encourage him to write out different endings for stories. Suggest he write a newsletter for relatives or neighbors.

Other ways to encourage creative writing are: keep a file of stories and poems your child writes, show him an interesting picture and have him write a story about it. You may want to consider sending off his best work to a children's magazine for publication. (A list of magazines that publish young people's writing is included in the appendix.) "Publication of early work is what a writer needs most of all in life," said novelist Erskine Caldwell. Also encourage journal-keeping, for the linguistically-gifted child will enjoy a chance to channel energy and ideas into a journal. All the language resources and reasons to write found in *Lifetime Writer* will encourage language talent.

You and your child can tape record your own stories when you travel. He can begin with, "Once when I was little..." or "My happiest birthday was..."

A typewriter or a word processor is a valuable tool at home. A public speaking course or a drama class for children would also be a good source of enrichment. Don't push or pressure, but follow your child's leading and do what he enjoys doing.

Musical Talent:

Musical talent, Dr. Gardner tells us, emerges earlier than any other intelligence.

From very early in life, Danny loved sounds. In a sense, you could say that he had a very fine-tuned tape recorder in his brain which was sensitive to music. Even as a little child, he could remember a song after having heard it only once. He learned new melodies quickly. He could imitate tone, rhythm, and melody.

The musically-gifted child often sings very well. He can pick out melodies by ear on the piano or other instrument, and loves to listen to music.

How can we encourage a child like Danny? We can play fine music in the home and in the car. Music teachers say that listening to classical music is best because the notes are not slurred and thus help children to develop the ability to discriminate pitch. As the child listens, ask him: "What kind of instrument is that?" Show him that you appreciate music. "I hear a flute and a violin. What do you hear? How does it make you feel — happy or sad?" That way the child is encouraged to begin to listen actively to music.

39

A younger musically-inclined child will enjoy a game in which you clap a rhythm pattern and he repeats it exactly as he hears it. Have a piano or other musical instruments available at all times. Piano lessons are a great way to start because they help the child to learn all the basics of rhythm, tone, harmony, and music theory. Carefully consider the maturity level and need of the child to determine the right age to begin his lessons. Avoid pressure and burnout which can sometimes accompany music lessons.

A computer program which allows your child to write and perform original music would be a great resource to have at home. With one program, "Songwriter," the child can experiment with time and melody to create single-voice compositions.

Take the child to symphonies, concerts and live musicals in your community. Let him be the songleader for family celebrations. If family is far away, make a tape recording of the child singing Christmas songs to send to a grandparent or an uncle.

When you look for a school for the child, find one that offers a broad range of music opportunities, such as band, orchestra, and chorus. Check with nearby colleges for special summer music camps or enrichment programs for musically-inclined children.

Spatial Ability:

The child who is spatially-gifted is an excellent visualizer. He thinks in pictures. Either by touching or seeing an object, he can picture it, imagine how it would look if it were turned around, and can visualize its relationship to other objects. He can see something one time and then reproduce it on paper very accurately.

Often the spatially-gifted child loves to draw. He can find his way between two places, put together hard puzzles, and is observant of detail.

Jack was such a child. He spent his childhood designing house plans and army equipment and is now an architect.

As a little girl, Patty spent hours making paper dolls and cutting out clothes from old pattern books which she color-coordinated. Today she is a clothing designer.

The spatial-talented child may also become a physicist, sculptor or painter. In order to develop his talent, he needs experiences in which he can use his imagination and be creative and inventive. He needs open situations in which there is no right or wrong way to make a snowman or erect a building. Provide him with art materials of all kinds: an easel, a variety of paper, tempera paint, brushes, markers, pastels or charcoal, and clay.

Collect old frames and give special drawings as gifts. Display his pictures on the family bulletin board. Have him design and make his own birthday party cards and invitations. Share creative activities with him. Find ways for his talents to serve your local church or community center. Let him help make posters for fund-raising projects or vacation Bible school. Provide him opportunities to create banners, or make a cover for the children's directory.

Games like checkers, chess, and three-dimensional tic-tac-toe are good for developing spatial reasoning. Practice interpreting maps can be lots of fun: help your child make a map of the neighborhood, complete with houses, signs and landmarks. Take him to art museums and a hands-on children's science museum. When you have family outings or go on field trips, have him take along a sketch book, pen and pencil to draw the statue or that historic bridge.

In addition, introduce him to computer programs like "Picturewriter" (ages 8-adult), a graphic arts tool for on-screen sketching, and "Paint," which offers experience in four-color painting on screen.

Bodily-Kinesthetic Talent

The child with this gift seems to have the ability to coordinate his muscle movements, operate with grace and timing and use his body and other objects with skill. He excels in activities requiring precision, power and speed. He may be talented in athletics, or gifted in dance.

The kinesthetically-gifted child may also display special motor skills for sewing or mechanical assembly. At an early age, he may be able to learn to ride a bike, do headstands, or take apart the family toaster and put it back together again. He may become an actor, gymnast, engineer or computer technician.

To encourage this gift, give the child plenty of athletic (large muscle) equipment, for both indoors and outdoors. Provide him opportunities to see a variety of dance performances or athletic contests, depending on his interest and enthusiasm. Let him join the YMCA swim team or pursue dance or the sport of his choice.

Provide Lego blocks and Erector sets for building. He may enjoy assembling model airplanes, ships or trains. Provide things to take apart and tinker with, purchased perhaps at a garage sale — an old clock, record player or small appliance. Encourage him to enter the science fair at school.

Engage in family craft projects. Give the child opportunities to participate in woodworking, needlework or calligraphy, if interested. The kinesthetically-talented child will love outings to real places of interest in your community, love to watch demonstrations of skills, and will especially enjoy hands-on science museums.

Summer sports camps will be a favorite of this type youngster. Drama classes or community college workshops in computers will also be a good resource.

This child may need extra help in some academic subjects in order to stay encouraged about school. Excelling in sports will be a highlight of his school years.

Logical-Mathematical Ability

Besides high scores on math achievement tests, the logical-mathematical child will show early computation skill. He will be fascinated by the order and pattern of objects. Often he will show intense concentration, be extremely curious, and good at problem-solving. He may look at big brother's algebra, understand the equations and show him how to solve the problems, even though the material is three grade-levels ahead of him. The budding scientist is marked, Gardner says, "by his ability to pose provocative questions and then follow them up with appropriate ones."[7]

If your young child has special logical-mathematical ability, give him opportunities to count, order and categorize. Maybe he can help you devise a better system for organizing a closet or garage. The Sesame Sreet Cookie Counter, a preschool electronic game, is both educational and lots of fun for this type youngster.

Math teacher Joyce Findley of Edmond, Oklahoma, advises that if a child is started on a computer too early in life and is not successful at it, he will lose interest. The games should not place too much pressure on the student, and the parent should not be overly competitive in his attitude; otherwise, the child will soon learn to avoid the game. Let him enjoy computer games, but find his own level of success at them.

He may enjoy solving "mental math problems" orally while riding along in the car. For example, teacher Shirley Pugh suggests that you ask him to figure out the answer to: 30 divided by 6 times 8 minus 2 plus 3 times 9.

See what enrichment programs your child's school offers for math-gifted students. With your encouragement, your child's math teacher may be persuaded to organize a math club to meet monthly. Mrs. Findley's high school math club plans a variety of activities: ancient games based on math computation; outside speakers such as an actuary, computer programmer, and engineer; math relays in teams. Participation in state and national math contests and exams, such as "Math Counts," a junior-high program, is also fun for mathematically-gifted children.

Provide games, such as Mastermind and Foursquare, which develop logic and mathematical skills. Also provide games, such as Battleship, Monopoly, chess and checkers, and math puzzle books which involve strategy and problem-solving.

Consider enrolling your child in a summer computer camp, or in one of the many summer programs offered by colleges for math/science-gifted children. Math teachers advise that parents make sure the child is not pressured to attend only because they want him to; he must decide to go because he thinks it will be fun.

The Personal Intelligences

Dr. Gardner describes the ability to know oneself and to know others as personal intelligence. The child gifted with the first type of personal ability perceives and verbalizes his own feelings well. "The core capacity at work here is *access to one's own feeling life* — one's range of affects or emotions: the capacity instantly to effect discriminations among these feelings, and eventually, to label them, to enmesh them in symbolic codes, to draw upon them as a means of understanding and guiding one's behavior."[8]

This child grows in understanding of himself and others. He has the ability to notice changes in others' moods, and to sense people's motives and feelings, which gives him great potential for social skills and leadership. As this potential is developed, he is able to communicate with, manage and organize people into action. He is very intuitive and has the ability to get along with the people around him, either at school or at work. He is sociable, and friendships remain a high priority for him throughout life.

In elementary years, he will enjoy games like Ungame, which involves communication and the sharing of feelings and ideas. Role-playing comes naturally for this child. To encourage him, provide him with costumes, hats and other dramatic play resources. Charades will be fun for a family evening together, and reading good literature aloud is also valuable.

Political and religious leaders, counselors and teachers share this kind of personal intelligence. To encourage it in your child, expose him to many vocations: let him spend a day observing a business executive or lawyer, or even work for one for a few weeks when he is old enough. Take him to the state legislature.

Provide him with a variety of rich language resources at home (see the section of this subject in Chapter 8 on reading and lifelong writing) so he will have opportunities to grow in communication skills.

Give him leadership opportunities working with people in the church youth group or organizing a neighborhood Christmas or summer block party. This child may enjoy participating in speech, debate and plays in school and community college workshops.

Most of all, *enjoy* your child and his gifts and talents. Provide opportunities to learn and bloom. Pay attention to your child's abilities, but don't let him go completely overboard in any one area. Children need balance and variety in their lives. If your daughter is precocious in reading and can recite poetry beautifully, but cannot skip and lacks physical coordination, involve her in games which help develop balance, coordination and timing. If your son is a great athlete, but is losing ground in academic subjects because of poor learning skills, find and invest in a tutor for him. The little math whiz needs to learn to enjoy reading for entertainment. Encouraging your child in one area should not be to the exclusion of all others.

Finally, allow your child unstructured time for play. Let him be a child, not a professional. Separate your aspirations and desires for success from your child's. Love unconditionally, independent of performance in the gifted area. Also praise your child for gifts of service, mercy, faith and encouragement of others.

As we help our children develop their talents, we further God's purpose in their lives.

Footnotes

[1]Marti Garlett, *Who Will Be My Teacher?* (Waco: Word Books, 1985), p. 125.

[2]James Dobson, *Hide or Seek: Self-Esteem for the Child* (Old Tappan: Fleming H. Revell, 1974), p. 71.

[3]From an interview in *Prevention* magazine, June 1985.

[4]Cliff Schimmels, *How to Help Your Child Survive and Thrive in Public School* (Old Tappan: Fleming H. Revell, 1982), p. 148.

[5]*What Works: Research About Teaching and Learning,* United States Department of Education, William J. Bennett, Secretary, 1986, p. 16.

[6]Howard Gardner, *Frames of Mind: The Theory of Multiple Intelligence* (New York: Basic Books, 1983).

[7]Ibid, p. 386.

[8]Ibid, p. 239.

Chapter 4

HOME ENVIRONMENT: THE NEED FOR STABILITY

Nathan was an enthusiastic kindergarten student. Then in first grade, before, during and after his parents' divorce, Nathan did not learn anything in school. He did not learn to read nor to do basic addition. He was too emotionally distraught. The climate in his home was too distracting, explosive and unpredictable for him to settle down to any kind of emotional security. Consequently, Nathan failed first grade and became a chronic behavior problem. It took two years of private tutoring and stabilizing of the home environment before Nathan was able to perform at grade level.

Is Nathan's home and school situation rare? No, say learning specialists. In fact, in many children what seems, on the surface, to be a learning disability is often evidence of a much deeper problem: anxiety and turmoil underneath.

"If there is turmoil in a child's heart or mind, it will cut learning as much as 90 percent. Researchers all over the country are saying the same thing: there is a very high correlation between anxiety and the inability to learn," says Dr. Dale Jordan of Jordan Diagnostic Center in Oklahoma City, Oklahoma.

Children must be able to concentrate and focus on what the teacher is saying and on the printed words or math problems in their texts. But often, they are unable to do so because they cannot turn off the inner conflict they bring with them to class.

Psychologist Dr. Diana Waters agrees: "Family instability and resulting inner turmoil interfere with the child's ability to perform and learn at school. Anxiety and depression both adversely affect a person's capacity for concentration and memory while at the same time lowering motivation for achievement. In general, the child expends much of his emotional and mental energy in dealing with his inner preoccupations."

A study of 4,000 seven-year-old children showed that chronic stress lowers IQ scores, not only in the immediate school situation but also developmentally for the child. The family, the researchers conclude, is clearly an important influence on children and their ability to learn.[1]

In some cases, school performance is maintained despite family instability, says Dr. Waters. In these cases, the child views the school arena as predictable, and channels his energies into school work as a way of warding off or isolating his feelings about his family.

Moreover, teachers also report that the most common classroom indicators of children who are experiencing disruption at home include: aggression toward peers, defiance toward authority, moodiness, daydreaming, withdrawal and declining grades. Such children experience low self-esteem, especially in regard to their capacity to master new tasks and adapt to unfamiliar situations. They also find it difficult to handle responsibility.[2]

Certainly, problems at home exercise a critical influence on the child at school. Family stability, therefore, is vital to a child's learning and achievement capacity.

What is Stability?

The dictionary defines *stability* as "not being easily moved or thrown off balance; not likely to break down, fall apart or give way; firm, steady, fixed, enduring; capable of returning to equilibrium or original position after being shaken or displaced."[3]

Sue Gouaux, a family counselor with Gouaux Clinical Associates, Inc. in St. Louis, likes to use the example of the family being like parts of a hanging mobile, with parents being the larger pieces and the children the smaller pieces. When external or internal stresses occur, the pieces move. They are all affected by the shifting motion of the others.

Difficult circumstances do come unannounced and uninvited into all of our lives. But what can we as parents do to *re-establish stability* when a crisis such as death, divorce, hospitalization or unemployment has shaken the family's security?

Re-establishing Stability in Times of Crisis

Rhana Robison, a counselor at the Family Life Center in Oklahoma City, Oklahoma, offers ways to re-establish stability when a crisis has shaken the family stability:[4]

"Consider the situation of Amy, age 7, a second grader," says Ms. Robison. "Shortly after her father left home and filed for divorce, Amy began to wet her bed and have accidents at school, causing her embarrassment. Concentrating on school work proved frustrating, and Amy began to get behind. Her mother had attempted to reassure Amy of her love, assuring her that she would never leave her. When the wetting continued, the mother sought out a child psychologist, who really gave her a source of support. She also had a good friend right around the corner, who allowed Amy to come visit whenever she wanted. This friend had a stable, happy home, and a listening ear, which gave Amy some time away from a grief-stricken mom. Gradually, Amy's wetting ceased, and she began to be happy at school and gain confidence again in her work."

Ms. Robison adds that children in the midst of a home torn by internal discord, divorce or death manifest their feelings in several ways: sadness, aggression, acting out, extreme withdrawal, return to bed-wetting, excessive crying and whining, failing grades, short attention span, daydreaming, headaches or stomachaches.

According to Ms. Robison, a child in this situation, needs several things:

1. Reassurance that the remaining parent will not leave him or quit loving him.

2. Outside, stable families or an extended family (grandparent, aunt) who love and accept him and who will offer times of respite. A support system for the child to add nurture and love to his life during a difficult time can make all the difference in the world in his ability to cope with his situation. Children can surmount so many more problems if they have a network of support.

3. Reassurance that he *did not* cause the separation, death or divorce. There needs to be honest, straight talk to relieve the child of guilt feelings of being responsible for the crisis or problem.

4. Attentiveness to his feelings. The child must be helped to put into words the feelings he is experiencing. He needs to know that it is okay for him to feel hurt, to be mad, to cry. If the parent doesn't have time to listen, he or she must find someone who does have the time.

5. Time for him to play and enjoy recreation. Exercise siphons off excess nervous energy and stress, and helps the child to cope.

6. A sense of order re-established in his life. A stable, structured environment restores a sense of security to the child in crisis. This structure should take the form of regular daily meals (with prayer and conversation), at least one of which needs to be taken as a family, as often as possible. The parent should establish regular hours for the child's sleeping and waking, studying, doing chores,

and playing. Stability needs to be established through fairly consistent, reasonable family rules and guidelines.

7. Professional help, if the problem warrants it.

Important Don'ts

If your child is exposed to a crisis situation:

1. Don't deny or ignore the symptoms of depression or overstress you see in him.

2. Don't be demanding; avoid limiting your communication with him to barking orders or applying pressure.

3. Don't withdraw from him; be accessible.

Parents should never be shy about requesting the support they need from friends, family, pastor, or counselor. Parents of a troubled child need to come to terms with their own feelings so these emotions are not played out through the child or dumped on him.

As the family re-establishes stability, Ms. Robison says, the child is helped to deal with the stress and changes brought on by a crisis situation. Then he can continue learning in the school setting without becoming overwhelmed or isolated.

Whatever our family situation, one of the greatest things we can do for our children is to let them know that we are *committed to them* for life: "I love you and will be here for you, no matter what happens."

This commitment is particularly important to a child's sense of security in a time of crisis, such as a job change, a family move or the death of a loved one. Also in times of the child's *own* development crises (such as adolescence), he needs to hear and know, "Whatever difficulties come our way, we are in this together, and we're going to make it!"

If the marriage has dissolved, commitment to the child is still an important stabilizing factor on the part of the parents. Children who have adjusted best are those who were free to love both parents and to develop affectionate relationships with stepparents.

A strong sense of commitment in the family builds a stable home base for the child and is an anchor that gives him the peace of mind and inner security he needs. Then he is free to concentrate on reading, writing, and other studies, to retain what he learns and to get the foundation he needs to succeed in school and in life.

Do We Have Time?

> "Love cannot be expressed without making time for the person whom we would love."
> Morton Kelsey
>
> *CARING: How Can We Love One Another?*[5]

Mom hurries in from work with a sack of groceries. Brian screeches by on his bike to deliver all the newspapers before dark. Upstairs, Sara hurriedly dresses for ballet class, then skips down the stairs three at a time to dash into the kitchen and ask, "Mom, can you buzz me to the dance studio?" At the same time, a tense Dad races home on the highway, muttering under his breath at anyone who gets in his way, knowing he will be home only 45 minutes before he has to preside at the Adult Education Committee at church.

Overcrowded lives — stressed parents — hurried children. Do you ever have a night like this? I do.

"I feel like I'm on a fast train and can't get off," one mother reports. "My life is all bits and pieces."

"I wish we had some time for Dad and me to go camping," ten-year-old Michael confides.

In many families today there is just not enough time. A recent headline noted that we Americans zoom through life in fast forward. Many parents report that they are continually tired, work too many hours, and can't figure out how to find more time.

Consequently, many of our nation's children lack what they need most — parents' time and attention. The average child, even in a two-parent home, gets about eight minutes of one-to-one time per week from either parent, and the great majority of that time is spent sending negative messages.

"We're amazed how many of these bright families we see that never have an evening meal together," says Dr. Dale Jordan. "If Mom fixes anything, it's laid out smorgasbord style, and whoever wants food can get it. They're running in all directions."

What happens to children in this fast-paced, harried family lifestyle? First, short-term memory is affected. Anxiety builds, blocking retention. If a child's short-term memory environment is jumbled and rushed, then his mind does not build long-term memory patterns. Outside stimulation diverts and usurps interior energy. It's like playing a 33-rpm record on 78-rpm speed — the child can't understand the meaning of what he hears. His mind becomes like a bowl of peanuts, just bits and pieces. He feels disorganized and alone. The combination of stress and hurry can rob him of vital reading, writing and math skills. In order to build a long-term framework of knowledge, there has to be a time when he is quiet, settled and reflective.

A Georgetown University study reveals that "reducing the level of stress in your family's life can raise your child's IQ."[6] One of the most important things we can do, then, for our children's education is to provide them a supportive family life and "to *be with them* in a non-conflictive environment in which there is a minimal amount of pressure, anger and hurry," said Dr. Jordan.

Giving your child some time in which your attention is focused on him alone, when you are truly "tuned in" to his needs, is a tangible way of showing him that he is worthwhile. It helps build self-esteem, establish communication and create emotional closeness. This "focused attention," as Dr. Ross Campbell, Associate Professor of Pediatrics and Psychology of the University of Tennessee, terms it, is a time to just enjoy each other, a time to set aside everything else (including our adult preoccupations and worries) in order to spend a few minutes just being together. Focused attention, says Dr. Campbell in his excellent book, *How to Really Love Your Child*, is the very best way to fill up a young person's emotional "tank."[7]

Focused attention may be a lunch together, or a short time to throw the football and talk over the events of the day. It can be a walk around the block or stopping for a Coke and a chat on the way home from soccer practice. The thirty minutes before bedtime is "prime time" to spend together. And this time of sharing and of focused attention needs to continue throughout the teenage years, keeping lines of communication open.

> Youngsters need focused attention most when they are under stress. The death or illness of a parent or grandparent, the arrival of a new baby, a divorce, a move, changes and disappointments, for example, are more bearable for youngsters if they have extra bits of I'm-all-here-for-you time.
>
> Charlotte Sawtelle
>
> *Learning Is a Family Affair*[8]

Dr. Jordan suggests that "the most important thing you can do for your child's education is to clear your calendar and be there during those formative years." He suggests that as many nights as possible, we come home in the evening, get relaxed, have a meal together, share the events of the day, have time for homework, reading and other shared activities.

We also need to help our children plan their time between work, play, study, sleep, family time and other activities so there is balance in their lives. When they are overscheduled and running from one activity to another, young people experience burnout just as adults do. Home becomes only a place where clothes are changed and a glass of milk is gulped down on the way out the door. Youngsters need to have some unstructured time for play, thinking or rest in the family setting.

All of our homes are busy, and mine can be as hectic as yours when two basketball games, a tennis match and play practice fall on the same day. But if it is our conviction that family time is important, then we will establish that as a priority. We will not let our own or our children's calendars become overscheduled. If we begin to be pulled in all directions, we will miss each other, because we will have learned to enjoy the closeness and support of family.

And we will cut back, if our schedules become overcrowded. We will make sure that our pace of life is productive, but not frenzied. Then our homes will be places of refuge and renewal for each family member. And we and our children will go out the next day with motivation and strength to tackle whatever lies ahead.

Dealing with School Stress

"School is hard for me. I get upset when I fail a test. I get real nervous when my teacher is mad at the class or when I do something wrong. I don't like to be called names (by the other pupils) or be left out of games at recess," said one fourth-grade boy.

We need to listen to our children talk about school, without interrupting them or criticizing — just listening. What are our kids saying about their school experience?

Lots of children are upset about things at school: afraid of being bullied on the bus or playground, fearful of being intimidated or humiliated by a teacher, frustrated at making low grades, bothered by problems with friends.

For some children school is a very positive, rewarding experience. But for others, the competitive, test-oriented atmosphere is stressful. Large classes are difficult. Children often feel as if they are being rushed from class to class, activity to activity throughout the school day. Many youngsters find classroom work repetitive, and monotonous; the stacks of worksheets stressful.

With increased emphasis on achievement and higher standards imposed in schools today comes more pressure. When more pressure is placed on them at school, children need correspondingly more support at home.

"We often put on more pressure than children can handle," says Dr. Eugene Walker, Director of Pediatric Psychology Training at the University of Oklahoma Medical School. "School teachers are putting on pressure. Parents are saying to their child, 'You can do better, you must bring your grades up,' and express displeasure when not satisfied with the results. At the same time parents are conveying displeasure with the child and their relationship with the child. Children have a hard time disconnecting their performance from who they are as people. Parents should try not to criticize and say, 'You have to do better.' They should promote and encourage, but not pressure."

He adds that for a while students seem to do better under pressure, but it soon gets tiresome, and they begin to experience burnout. Unless something is done to relieve the stress, they will eventually quit trying and drop out. Many capable students do great in elementary school — they turn in perfect papers, receive top grades, take pride in accomplishment; but then in high school and college, they deteriorate.

According to a report entitled "Young Adolescents and Their Parents," issued by a leading research institute and based on the responses of more than 8,000 students in grades five through nine, the children's main worry was how they were doing in school. Next, they worried about their looks; then, about how their friends treated them; and finally, about being a victim of sexual abuse or assault.

Parents need to listen to their children and discover the issues that distract them from learning. If your child seems troubled, ask questions like: What's going on at school? What are you interested in? What is difficult about school? Do you have any enemies at school? How do they make you feel? Are you having any problems in your classwork? What are your happiest times at school?

"Total empathy is difficult to achieve, and no one can empathize with another person all the time. When we can, however, it means a great deal to our children. 'Mom understands.' 'Dad understands.' It feels good to be understood. It wipes out loneliness."

Charlotte Sawtelle

Learning Is a Family Affair[9]

After we listen to the particular worries of our children, we can show empathy and understanding, without condemning or judging. We can be physically supportive (with hugging or holding). We can give information and share feelings. We can let our children know that we are with them in their problems. We can let them know that we had the same kind of problems when we were young. We can share our past experiences and struggles with them, and say, "This happened to me, and I still made it through, and so can you." We can suggest alternatives or offer to provide any extra help that may be needed. We may decide to schedule a conference with a teacher or school counselor.

If there is a learning gap or an academic deficiency causing low grades or failure, a tutor may be able to help the child catch up. Many times enormous strides can be made by one-to-one tutoring.

Commitment, stability, and time together — these are some of the greatest gifts we can give our children, creating a network of support they need to learn and succeed in school and life.

Recommended Reading

Briggs, Dorothy Corkhill. *Your Child's Self Esteem*. New York: Doubleday, 1970.

Campbell, Ross. *How to Really Love Your Child*. New York: Signet Books, 1982.

Green, Holly Wagner. *Turning Fear to Hope*. New York: Thomas Nelson Publishers, 1984.

Leman, Kevin Dr. *Making Children Mind Without Losing Yours*. Old Tappan: Fleming H. Revell, 1984.

Smalley, Gary. *The Key to Your Child's Heart*. Waco: Word Books, 1984.

Footnotes

[1]*Science Digest* (Oct. 1983), p. 78.

[2]"Family Problems: How They're Affecting Today's Classrooms" *Learning 86*, Vol. 14, No. 5, (Jan. 1986).

[3]*Webster's New World Dictionary of the American Language* (New York: Collins World, 1974), pp. 1416,1417.

[4]The author is indebted to Rhana Robison for her suggestions on re-establishing stability.

[5]Morton Kelsey, *CARING: How Can We Love One Another?* (New York: Paulist Press, 1981), p. 103.

[6]*Science Digest* (Oct. 1983), p. 78.

[7]Ross Campbell, *How to Really Love Your Child* (New York: Signet Books, 1982).

[8]Charlotte Sawtelle, *Learning Is a Family Affair* (Maine Department of Educational and Cultural Services: 1984), p. 10.

[9]Ibid, p. 17.

Chapter 5

HOW TO "TURN ON" YOUR PRESCHOOLER TO LEARNING

Debbie, the mother of a bright, active four-year-old boy, Brian, came to me in a quandary. "All Brian does is watch television," she said. "His friend across the street moved, and now he sits for hours in front of He-Man and SuperFriends cartoons when he gets home from preschool. I have the baby to take care of, dinner to prepare, sewing, laundry and other chores to juggle, so I just can't entertain him all the time. Yet I'm troubled about the hours he wastes watching television. What can I do?"

Debbie is right to be concerned. The most critical time of intellectual development is the period *before* five years of age — when the foundation is being laid for all later skills: reading, writing, reasoning, math and communication.

Yet American preschoolers spend more of their waking hours watching television than any other age group: 54 hours per week. Watching television is a passive pastime that:

- stifles children's creativity

- shortens their attention span

- stunts their language ability

- deprives them of conversation, questions and physical activity

By the end of their kindergarten years, many children have already watched 5,000 hours of television!

In addition, psychologists report that children are experiencing tremendous stress from the visual overload of too much television viewing, including such damage as inner-ear problems, nearsightedness, and increased aggressive behavior. We must provide alternatives for our children!

Like Brian's mom, you may be very busy keeping up with your job, doing housework, carpooling, and caring for your child's siblings. He may be in preschool or a mother's day out program, but during his hours at home, how can your child's time be better spent than watching TV?

Here are some ways which will help you encourage your child to discover the joy of learning, develop readiness skills in a non-pressured atmosphere, and meet his needs developmentally. These activities will also benefit the elementary-age child and can be done with a parent, grandparent, older sibling, or caretaker.

Pretend Play:

Educators are re-discovering the value of pretend play as a vital part of children's learning processes. Contrary to what we may think as adults, pretend play is not a waste of time. We often think it's just play, that children can and should drop it at a moment's notice. Or we may even discourage them from pretending at all. However, pretend play is essential to children's growth and learning. It encourages the development of language, vocabulary and communication skills. In fantasy play, children come to realize that one thing can stand for another, a background for understanding words as symbols (reading) and numbers as symbols (math).

Pretend play helps children learn to deal with fears and difficult situations, and increases their emotional stability. Fantasy play develops creativity. It fosters confidence in solving problems, as children think, plan and carry out an idea.

Pretend play is a symbol system, a way for children to represent reality, says Dr. Margaret Loeffler, Primary Director of Casady School in Oklahoma City, Oklahoma. We can encourage pretend play by providing our children with costumes, props and toys *and* by allowing our preschoolers enough *time* to play in an unhurried atmosphere.[1]

Here are some costumes, props and toys that stimulate pretend play:

- dress-up clothes, long garments, Grandma's old costume jewelry and accessories, vests, ties

- hats of many shapes and sizes — fireman's hat, straw hat, cowboy hat, glamorous hat, baseball cap, grandfather's hat

- medical kits, props for playing hospital, Ace bandages

- travel props — tickets, tour guide book, small suitcase, purse, old camera, play money

- office props — old or play telephone, adding machine, receipt book, old typewriter

- dolls and all their play accessories

- big blocks and building toys, big refrigerator box for playing house

- stuffed animals

- puppets — homemade or bought (great language builders and drama resources), materials to make a backdrop or a box to make a stage

- blanket or sheet to put over a table to make a "tent"

- flannel board with bright pieces of felt in many different shapes and colors to use to create scenes and retell stories

- colorforms

Dr. Loeffler also suggests that along with these pretend-play resources we include pencils and paper to motivate our children to want to learn to read and write, as they are encouraged to incorporate literature into their fantasy play. If they are playing office, they can write pretend letters. While playing school, they can make a list of their pupils. Playing house calls for the making of a grocery list. Your child may want to imitate your vocation in his or her pretend play.

To take full advantage of the costumes, props and toys provided them, children need access to a space they don't have to keep picked up all the time. They need to be able to spread out and "re-create" their own play space.

By providing them these opportunities and this freedom of expression, we give our children permission to play, says Dr. Loeffler, so they can take the initiative to play the way they need to. Children who are made to feel guilty about "wasting time" or "messing up the house" with their pretend play do not develop that initiative. As we observe their uninhibited pretend play, we can see what our children are thinking about and talking about. This provides us valuable insights into their interests, gifts and personalities. After they have had time to play in an unrestrained atmosphere, then we can set a reasonable time for them to pick up and return to normal living patterns.

Last, we need to give our preschoolers enough *time* to enagage in pretend play. Often we overschedule children with outside activities — music class, gymnastics, preschool and church activities — until they never have time to develop initiative in play.

Overscheduling interferes with the time and freedom children need to develop to the fullest their ability to imagine and create.

Amazing Art Box:

Have accessible to your child an art box in a plastic container. A cabinet by the kitchen table is a good place to keep it. Be sure to include a plastic placemat for him to put down in case of spills.

Pencils and paper are vital. The best readers, writers and artists of today were "pencil-and-paper kids" who spent a lot of their preschool years scribbling and drawing at home.[2]

Also include in the art box:

- crayons, washable markers
- fingerpaints
- safe scissors, a glue stick, bright catalogs and magazines (to cut pictures from)
- brightly-colored construction paper
- stickers of cats and clowns, Santas, bells, musical notes, balloons (and whatever else your child fancies)
- scraps of fabric, wallpaper, strings and buttons (to use to make collages)
- different colors of playdough (homemade or purchased)
- modeling clay

At least *once a day*, suggest to your child: "Let's get out your art box and make something!" Let the child's interests lead. If he is currently fascinated with dinosaurs, lead in that direction. If firemen and firetrucks capture his interest at present, ask him to draw a picture of a brave rescue. Or say: "It's art time. Why don't we get out some construction paper and stickers and make a get-well card for Grandma who's in the hospital."

Art time can be as varied as your imagination. One day it can consist of listening to a story tape like "The Selfish Giant" and illustrating the story. Another day pretend food can be made out of play dough for the child's dolls to partake of at a later tea party.

Remember to *encourage* your artistic child by *displaying* what he creates, perhaps by affixing it to the refrigerator door with a magnet, or by granting it a special place of honor on the family bulletin board.

When, at age five, our son, Chris, used a ruler and various colored pencils to create a picture of the "Steadfast Tin Soldier," whom he heard about in a children's story, we framed his work of art and hung it in the living room. His aunts liked it so much they asked him to draw a Steadfast Tin Soldier for them to display in their homes. What an encouragement to Chris' budding interest in art!

Take the time to show an active interest in your child's artistic efforts and creations: "How did you mix that red and blue together so smoothly in the rainbow? I like the way you drew the grass in short, choppy strokes."

Games for Learning:

Each day, have someone in the family play one simple, age-appropriate simple board game with your child. Whenever possible, stretch out on the carpet with him yourself, relax and enjoy a game together. Younger preschoolers won't understand complicated rules, but a game such as Memory (players use their memory to locate and collect matching pairs of picture cards), one of our children's favorites, improves memory and visual discrimination.

A short board game can teach your child many new concepts and can help develop skills he will need later in classroom learning. Chutes and Ladders was one of our family favorites. It develops visual discrimination and social skills, as well as counting abilities. Candy Land, for ages 4 and up, is good for the development of visual discrimination. The Scrabble Alphabet Game is great fun and provides pre-reading practice for preschoolers.

Playing games is also an enjoyable way to foster communication, and are effective learning aids as long as parents and children *enjoy* playing them together. We need to be patient while our children are learning the rules to the game. We must not accuse them of cheating when rules are too complicated for them to fully understand.

Bars, Balls and Balance:

Preschoolers need resources for physical development, so we need to provide large-muscle exercisers both inside and outside our homes. Our preschooler loved the small Nerf basketball and goal which fit on a door and gave him something to do with his boundless energy on rainy days. (He's thirteen now and still plays with it!) Here are some resources for your preschooler's physical activity:

- playground equipment (like a geodesic dome) for climbing, a swing set (either in your yard or at a nearby playground)

- balance beam (which you can make yourself with cement blocks and a sturdy board)

- riding toys

- horseshoes, beanbag toss, pounding toys

- chinning bar (which fits on a doorway and can be adjusted to your child's height)

- rebounder (a small indoor trampoline — a great investment! Let your child jump to his favorite music. Learning clinics use rebounders to increase neurological connections needed for intellectual development; plus, jumping is a lot of fun)

- music exercise tapes and video exercise programs for kids (such as Mary Lou Retton's "Fun and Fitness")

- balls of all sizes

Your child will also enjoy toys such as puzzles that stimulate small-muscle development. One family I know keeps a puzzle out on the coffee table each day for the children to work on. Another mother is helping her four-year-old learn the states by using a large 50-state wooden puzzle map. They tie each state in with an idea and alternate questions and answers with the states. For example, the mother begins the game:

Q. "Point to the state where your cousin lives. Name it, take out the state piece."

A. "Arkansas."

Q. "Where do they grow potatoes?"

A. "Idaho."

Then the daughter asks the mother questions about the states.

Shape sorters, Legos, blocks and construction toys are all good small-muscle toys. Blocks are the ideal toy and contribute to almost every aspect of a child's learning, especially math.

Someone's in the Kitchen with Mother:

There are lots of opportunities for your child to learn math and weight-volume concepts and to engage in simple science experiments in the kitchen (with a little ingenuity and lots of patience on your part).

As you work in the kitchen, use specifics when you talk to your child. For example, say, "Here are three grapes for you," and then count them out to him one at a time. Ask him, "Do you want your sandwich cut into halves or fourths?" showing him the difference with your own sandwich.

Teach your child to follow a simple recipe. He can make his own pudding (with a little help from you). You can read the recipe step by step, and your child can help measure, stir and, of course, lick the bowl. Along the way, talk about what you are doing.

Some Saturdays, one busy mother, Debbie Bouziden, gives her daughter the choice of making pudding or watching Saturday cartoons. And making pudding always wins out! Mother and daughter have the pudding for dessert at lunchtime that day.

There are many great cookbooks for children on the market today. Most of these books have large, easy-to-read letters and simplified instructions and colorful illustrations.

While you cook, let your child string together different colors of macaroni. This exercise helps develop muscle and hand-eye coordination. As you prepare a dish, ask your child, "What does this smell like? What do you think it will taste like?"

For a simple science experiment, let your child mix oil and water (in a clear container, not on the kitchen counter!) and watch them separate. Then talk about why this strange occurrence takes place.

Let him count cookies as he puts them on the plate for you. As you allow your child to help you measure, he begins to understand weight and volume concepts.

Who's Afraid of the Big Bad Wolf?

Before bedtime, read a story to your child. Don't just read it; discuss it. Ask, "What do you think might happen now?" Active reading and listening will bring your child countless benefits later in the form of improved comprehension skills. It will build in him a desire to read and will contribute toward the development of a positive attitude toward books. Give him "wordless" picture books which he can "read" to himself to relax before naptime. These creative books tell a well-developed story in pictures, while boosting your preschooler's language and imagination skills.

Reading with your preschooler can take place any time — in the doctor's office or the family kitchen. One busy mother of five has her children read to her (and their preschool siblings) while she is preparing a meal or folding clothes.

Provide interesting books and magazines around your house that are appropriate for your preschooler. Jim Trelease's *The Read-Aloud Handbook* and Gladys Hunt's *Honey for a Child's Heart* contain excellent lists of children's books for each age group.[3]

"Kindergarten children who know a lot about written language usually have parents who believe that reading is important and who seize every opportunity to act on that conviction by reading to their children," say reading experts.[4] That may mean getting up thirty minutes early to spend time with your child, as one working mother does, or putting everything aside for ten minutes at the end of the day to curl up on the bed beside your youngster to share a book.

In addition to reading, *tell stories*. Storytelling motivates young children to read. In addition, "Storytelling also introduces them to cultural values and literary traditions before they can read, write, and talk about stories by themselves."[5]

Children are never bored with storytelling; it instills in them a desire to learn and sparks their imagination. You can tell your own version of classic fairy tales, Bible stories, accounts of your escapades as a child, or just fantasy stories. You can share from the great storehouse of family lore, recounting your Aunt Jane's great adventure in China, the tale of Grandpa's first Model-T, the story about the time, at eighteen months of age, you jumped into the lake dressed in your Easter finery. Storytelling can take place anywhere you and your children happen to be. Preschoolers are enchanted by storytelling, and learn vital listening skills in the process.

Communicate:

Recently, while I was sitting at a table in our local library doing research, a mother and two children came in the door. As the mother casually chatted with the librarian, her little girl, who was around three or four years of age, listened politely. During a pause in the adult conversation, she looked up eagerly and said, "Did you know I got a bike for my birthday?"Several times she posed her question, but no one was listening.

"My cat ran away; I miss my kitty," the little girl said — but still no response. With a look of sadness on her tiny face, she finally turned and aimlessly wandered away.

Often we tell our preschool children not to interrupt, but the truth is that many times they can't get a word in at all!

We can stimulate our children's interest in reading, writing and the world around them by answering their seemingly endless questions: Why is the moon round? Why is my hair red? Where does bread come from?

One mother said she tries to answer her child's questions as completely and honestly as possible. She uses her normal vocabulary and explains in as much detail as she can in order to provide a great deal of verbal input. Her child then begins to use new words in her own sentences. By conversing intelligently with her young daughter, this mother has provided her with a broad base of verbal and linguistic knowledge.

Engaging in conversation with your preschooler is one of the most important things you can do to help him develop language skills. Talk to him when you are together, and listen to him. According to the United States Department of Education, American mothers spend eight to fifteen minutes a day talking or explaining to their children. Fathers spend even less. Yet conversation is one of the most important means of developing language capability.

Conversation is a low-cost way to provide your child speaking and listening skills that will help him succeed in and out of the classroom.

Tape-recording Fun:

A tape recorder can be one of the best friends a busy mother ever had! Here are some ways to use the tape recorder to enhance your child's learning:

- Your preschooler can dictate stories into the tape recorder — perhaps his own rendition of The Three Bears, or a purely made-up story.

- If your child is away from you for day care, or for a weekend, he can take along his own tape recorder (an easily operated one such as the Fisher-Price model) and at naptime he can listen to a story you have pre-recorded. The auditory stimulation is good, and hearing your voice is also reassuring, reminding him that Mom still exists and still cares about him.

- One mother found that teaching Bible verses to her two- and three-year-olds is easier when she first reads the verse in context out of the Bible. Then the children repeat the verse as she says it. Next they record the verse separately (each child in his turn) and then read the verse out of the Bible once more. Finally, they play the tapes back for themselves in order to review. (Children love hearing the sound of their own voices.) This mother has found that her children can memorize about two verses a week using the tape recorder.

- There are many activity-music tapes available today which are great outlets for the energetic preschooler. You can take music tapes along on trips and let your child listen and sing along as he rides in the car.

- Many stories and books for children are now on tape. Story tapes make long trips much more enjoyable. Your child can also listen to a story in the kitchen while you cook dinner or do the dishes. (See the appendix for a list of tape resources.)

Love Notes:

Even before he can read all the words, begin to write notes to your child combining easy words he can recognize with pictures. In doing so, you create a rebus message perfect for the pre-reader to figure out. "I ♥ you!" written on the napkin in his lunch box can brighten up his day. He is reminded of your love and his curiosity about language is stimulated at the same time. Then as he grows, he will begin to surprise you with little notes of his own, like the one I received one morning years ago from my son, Chris:

"MOM — I LOVE miy mom and miy mom love me.
LOVE Chris"

It seems like only yesterday, and I still treasure the note!

Your child can put reminders on the bulletin board, or dictate a thank-you note to Grandma or Grandpa for the birthday present. Later, letter writing will come more naturally for your child and he will enjoy writing more because of these early opportunities provided for him at home.

When your child does try to sound out words in his at-home attempts at writing, encourage him in the "invented spelling" he uses rather than discouraging him by criticizing his less-than-perfect efforts or by changing his spelling. As his reading vocabulary grows through elementary school, his spelling vocabulary will also expand.

Outings and Walks:

Outings and walks are a good way to open your child's eyes to the world around him and provide unlimited resources for learning. There are fire-station outings and bus-ride outings, as well as outings to the television station, bakery, museum, aquarium, construction site, and post office.

What a great resource the public library is! On your way to do errands, or on a special Saturday outing, stop by the library with your child. You will be amazed at the myriad of library programs offered right in your community for children of all ages, but especially for preschoolers: drama, storytelling, puppetry, even toddler aerobics! Before you leave the library, let your child check out some books, art prints, stories on tape, or educational toys.

Candy Snowbarger, mother of four boys under age six (including twins) plans the most creative walks:

- Sticky-tape walks: place masking tape around the child's wrists with the sticky side out. In autumn, look for signs of fall and put those on the tape. When you get home, make a collage of what you have found.

- Theme walks: search for different types of houses, trees, clouds. These are good walks to practice counting things.

- Smelly walks: smell as you go and determine what you are smelling.

- Color walks: find all red things on the walk. Next day find all the yellow things around your block.

"Not only do we see and learn so much on these walks," says Candy, "but the boys and I have great conversations."

A variation on the color walks are "color days." Have a "red day" in which you: dress in red clothes, eat red food, talk about "r-words" or words with "red" in them, color or paint with red, find all the red toys in the house, say "My favorite red things are...," make a red collage with pictures cut from magazines, sing "Who is wearing red today?" (to the tune of "Here We Go Round the Mulberry Bush").

Limit TV Time!

Your preschooler won't have time to engage in these activities if he is glued to the television set. So limit his TV viewing. Educators say that preschoolers should be allowed to watch *no more* than one hour of television a day.

If your child has a babysitter or is in day care, check with his caretaker to see how much television viewing is included in his daily schedule. Some centers and in-home caretakers rely far too heavily on television babysitting. If this is the case with your caretaker, express your concern and suggest other activities which provide the interaction and development your child needs.

At home, decide with your preschooler at the first of the week the most valuable programs to watch during the next seven days. Make him a schedule with pictures to represent the shows he can watch, and tack it up on the bulletin board or affix it to the refrigerator where he can easily see it. If possible, watch a program with your child and discuss it. *When the show is over, turn the set off.*

One night a parent asked me, "If I limit television time, won't I have three faces staring at me expecting entertainment? Won't they drive me crazy?"

As a matter of fact, the opposite will be true. When we took the television out of our home for three months, our children actually learned to be more creative and entertained themselves better than ever before. They got out games and toys they hadn't played with for months; they talked more and spent more time drawing pictures and writing. An old jump rope, discarded from summer, was put back into use; Legos came out of the closet. The children were even more willing to help fold clothes alongside me or to put away silverware from the dishwasher when they weren't afraid of missing a re-run of "Happy Days."

Time? These activities do take some time, but it is time well spent. Remember that the thirty minutes you spend with your child investigating a spider spinning a web, as he asks questions and you share what you know, plants valuable seeds. Maybe later you can get a book about spiders from the library or read to your child an article on the subject from the encyclopedia. Then you might encourage him to draw a picture of a spider or to make up a story about one. As you follow the leading of your child's interest and your own intuition, this time becomes more valuable in terms of helping your child become a lifelong learner than a whole day in an ordinary school setting.

Last, to wisely guide our preschoolers, we need to know more about child development. Often parents don't understand what children at a certain age really are like, how they think, what they are capable of doing and learning. Thus they often expect inappropriate behavior from their children. They may expect too little of them in some areas, and too much in others. Because a child speaks well, for example, his parents may think he knows and understands much more than he really does. So the child is hurried to be an adult and too much emotional maturity is expected of him.

Sometimes as parents we forget that our three- and four-year-olds are just that, little children. Often we expect far too much of them — and ourselves. Reading and gaining an understanding of child development is important if we are to make the right decisions about what is appropriate for our children at each age level. The information below may be helpful in this area.

What we modern-day Americans tend to do, says Dr. Loeffler, is to see one age as the "staging age" for the next, rather than *seeing what the child should be doing and enjoying at that age.* When the child is in kindergarten, we sometimes act as though we are getting him ready for first grade. Years ahead of time, we begin thinking of his getting into college. Instead, we need to learn to enjoy the precious preschool years with our children, and to allow them to unhurriedly enjoy those years too.

One mother asked me, "But will my child be learning what he is supposed to and be prepared for kindergarten? Should I be doing workbooks with him?" Then she went on to express her underlying concern, "I'm not sure I'm doing the right things at home."

As a parent, you may be experiencing that same concern. If so, let me assure you of one thing: If you are giving your child reasons and resources to play and learn, adding your own interests and creative ideas, if you are encouraging him in his efforts (not pushing or pressuring him), then you have no need to fear for your child's future or his preparation to face it. As a result of your guidance and encouragement, a whole world of discovery and wonder will be open to him. A foundation will have been laid for vital school skills. And, most of all, you can be confident that he will become *a lifelong learner*, ready for all the challenges which lie ahead.

Footnotes

[1]The author is indebted to Dr. Margaret Loeffler for her insights on pretend play.

[2]*What Works: Research About Teaching and Learning,* United States Department of Education, William J. Bennett, Secretary, 1986, p. 14.

[3]Jim Trelease, *The Read-Aloud Handbook* (New York: Penguin Books, 1986) and Gladys Hunt's, *Honey for a Child's Heart* (Grand Rapids: Zondervan, 1974).

[4]*What Works,* p. 9.

[5]*What Works,* p. 25.

Chapter 6

HOMELIFE: THE KEY TO READING SUCCESS

How to Produce a Child with Reading Disabilities

Karen Gale, a reading specialist at Remedial Reading Resources in Edmond, Oklahoma, and I talked about her work tutoring children and adults in reading.

"From our screening, I see a real pattern among children with reading disabilities," she observed. "The home environment has very busy parents who have little time for the children, and who do very little reading themselves. There is no reading aloud in the home. They are very entertainment-oriented with television, videos and movies receiving top priority.

"In fact," she concluded, "if parents want to encourage poor reading skills, they should do all these things!"

Her observations came after teaching hundreds of children and adults to read. She pointed out that over half the school children in the United States are categorized as "deficient readers," noting that the family environment has a tremendous impact upon a child's reading ability.

Why Is Reading So Important?

Learning specialists say that *reading is the most important of all study skills.* This is true not just for the English class, but also for history, science, and math (especially in understanding math concepts and word problems). In fact, almost 90 percent of all school work requires reading. After the third grade, all school subjects depend on language. So it is critical that children become good readers.

Spelling and grammar abilities are directly related to reading experience. The development of listening skills is a vital benefit of being read to.

> "Research shows a strong connection between reading and listening. A child who is listening well shows it by being able to retell stories and repeat instructions. Children who are good listeners in kindergarten and first grade are likely to become successful readers by the third grade. Good fifth-grade listeners are likely to do well in aptitude and achievement tests in high school."
>
> *What Works*[1]

Critical thinking and imagination flow out of reading time; in addition, writing and speaking abilities are a function of the amount and quality of reading. Vocabulary development is enhanced by reading; business leaders point to the relationship of high vocabulary to success in *any* field.

Reading, then, is a door to learning, and all our efforts should be aimed toward the goal of producing motivated, lifelong readers.

Homelife Is the Key

From each new million-dollar research study the same message is coming forth — *home life is the key to reading*. As the prime factor in determining reading success, the National Assessment of Education Progress Report (released in September, 1985) targeted home environments that:

- encourage reading with an abundance of interesting materials
- place limits on television viewing
- emphasize homework completion

The researchers studied a quarter of a million American students from ages nine through seventeen. They concluded that even more important than the child's IQ or the type of innovative reading program used at his school, it is his *home* that makes the greatest difference in his reading ability.

Millions of dollars are being spent each year in an attempt to teach our children to learn to read at school. Yet this tremendous spending is in vain if our young people do not develop the desire to read at home where they can be given the practice necessary to become fluent readers. Just as an athlete's physical muscles must be exercised persistently if he is to develop strength for the game, so the student's reading "muscles" need to be exercised at home. Beginning with a good foundation, gained by learning to read in the early grades, he needs to continue to develop speed and comprehension skills so that in eleventh grade when Emily Bronte's *Wuthering Heights* (or another senior high school book) is assigned, he will be able to read, understand and respond to it.

Beyond that, we want our children to read not just because they have to, but in order to develop a love for reading which will then provide them a lifetime of enjoyment.

Reminders for the First Five Years

Most of us would agree that children learn more in the first five years than during any other time period in their lives. Since language development begins at home, the International Reading Association's pamphlet, "Your Home Is Your Child's First Home,"[2] provides parents excellent reminders of what to do to help foster reading development during these crucial first five years of life:

- help the child feel wanted and loved

- encourage self-reliance

- teach the child to listen attentively and follow directions

- talk to the child from birth, softly, gently, lovingly, but don't use baby talk

- answer questions

- teach an awareness of things

- help the child develop self-expression

- give the child correct names for things

- read to the child regularly

- build up a background of experiences

All of these at-home activities are much more effective than formal workbooks in building a foundation for reading. The most likely-to-succeed readers are those who come to first grade very familiar with the written word. In fact, reading makes more sense and has more value for the child who *writes* early. Letting your child dictate stories to you before he can write the letters of the alphabet is worthwhile. Then he can easily make the transition from spoken to written language which reading entails.

Unfortunately, after the child begins school, many times his parents will abdicate their position of responsibility for his development. Instead of remaining closely involved with his education, they will begin to look to the school to provide his reading experiences. But in the average elementary school, children spend only seven or eight minutes a day reading silently. Often there are so many activities in their daily schedule there is little read-aloud time. During the middle years, many children lose interest in reading if that interest is not kept alive at home.

Instilling a Love of Reading

There are many simple, inexpensive things you can do at home to improve your child's reading ability, and thus the quality of his whole education. At the top of the list is to *read yourself!*

Because one of the major learning methods of children is imitation, your role model alone can instill a love of reading in your child. If you don't like to read, look at your past school experiences and work through your negative attitudes. Find *something* you would like to know more about, then take time and read about it. Don't say to your child, "You'll never be very good in reading; I wasn't." Poor reading is not a disease your child can catch. But you do pass along your habits and attitudes concerning reading.

We can share our interests with our children. If they see that reading books, magazines, and newspapers is a natural part of our lives, they will likely welcome reading as a natural part of their lifestyle too.

Reading Resources

Next, provide a variety of reading resources at home and help each child find his own particular areas of interest. I am constantly amazed at how *different* and unique each child's reading interests are, but I am also convinced that we can find *something* that each one will enjoy reading about, if we look hard enough.

Our oldest son likes compelling fiction and mysteries, war stories and history. In contrast, our son, Chris, likes to read encyclopedias, statistics about the rainfall of Nebraska or NFL football teams. He devours the sports page of the daily newspaper and loves biographies of sports heros. Alison likes to read about girls in gymnastics, ballet and the fifth grade. She loves biographies of famous women such as Helen Keller, Harriet Tubman and Clara Barton.

The library has always been a terrific resource for discovering these individual interests. Every two weeks we trekked to the library to stock up on reading material and to give each child an ever-changing supply of books. We spent enough time for each child to come to feel at home there and to be able to look for books on his own. With time to browse, the children always found books I never would have thought of! You can also find and make available books that will interest your children.

Then, when we came home, I found *visible, accessible* places for the books to be placed — in a big basket by our easy chair, on the coffee table, on a shelf by the children's beds, in the car on trips. For youngsters, what is out of sight is truly out of mind, so books need to be in a highly visible spot. (At our house, the televison set, however, sits behind the closed doors of a cabinet.)

Also, develop your own personal library at home. One of our best investments has been a good set of encyclopedias. An atlas and reference books, children's classics, and a set of fairy tales can be included. You can give books as gifts at Christmas and birthdays, with a loving inscription in the front. A gift subscription to a bookstore with a good children's section is a real treat. Enroll your child in a book club suited to his age and interests.

Magazines offer great reading motivation for young people of all ages. Through the pre-teen and teenage years, when so many activities and people fill our children's time, magazines are a good way to continue steering them toward reading for personal enjoyment. Our children enjoy reading *National Geographic, World Tennis, Highlights for Children, Reader's Digest,* and *Guideposts.* Once a year their generous grandmother gives each of us a subscription to a favorite magazine. There are outdoor magazines, computer magazines, sports magazines — one for just about every imaginable area of interest.

Outings and Hobbies

You can build a background of experiences by providing regular family outings and encouraging hobbies. An outing to a place of interest to your child can stimulate his desire to read. For example, you have a half-day outing to the aquarium, and your child is curious about the eels and sting rays. So you follow up by sharing a colorful book on sea life which you borrow from the library. Camping, the county fair, Octoberfest and other local festivals, theater centers, bird and wildlife sanctuaries, museums — the list of outing possibilities is endless.

The favorite yearly outing of one of our boys was a trip to the 45th Army Infantry Museum. That led to his reading army history and pouring over books on army equipment, uniforms and weaponry. Drawing tanks, army vehicles and uniforms followed. One thing does lead to another when a child pursues an interest and natural learning takes place.

Moreover, be attentive to discern a hobby your child might want to pursue. A hobby can give your youngster a great reason to read about collecting baseball cards, stamps or coins; building model airplanes or rockets; gardening; woodworking; bird watching; sewing; or cooking.

Support your child's hobbies. Help him find sources to which he can write for information and supplies. Go to the library with him to find books on the hobby. Build on your child's hobbies, and he will have a great built-in reading resource.

So, search! Facilitate your child's reading! Consider yourself his best resource person — you know him better than anyone and can help find areas of interest, and books to match them. You will go a long way toward encouraging learning if you can get your child "hooked on" books at a young age, and then keep that interest going.

Other resources in your home — even in the kitchen — offer great possibilities. As you cook, for instance, let your child read the recipe to you. Buy a children's cookbook and encourage his or her culinary efforts. Have one child find an unusual word in the dictionary and then quiz the family on it at dinner. Share an interesting fact from the encyclopedia. Clip interesting newspaper or magazine articles on current issues to discuss at the table. Rotate the family devotional or Bible reading so each person in the home has a turn to read and lead discussion.

Travel and Reading

Travel is a great family resource that encourages reading. In planning a trip, write for brochures in advance and assign each member of the family points of interest you will be visiting. Each person will then read up on the particular landmarks or historic sites assigned to him. When the family arrives at a certain destination, the person who has "read up on it" will serve as the family "tour guide" and share all he has learned about it.

Listening to books recorded on cassette is a good way to pass the time on long trips. You can have a read-aloud time once a day to break up the nine hours or so you will be spending daily in the car.

Reading Aloud in the Family

In the fall and winter when dark comes early and the cold wind rages, our children particularly loved snuggling up to the fireside in sleeping bags and listening while Dad read a favorite series, one chapter a night. (Laura Wilder's *Little House on the Prairie* books and C.S. Lewis' *Chronicles of Narnia* were all-time favorites.)

When Can You Find the Time?

As a busy parent, when can you find the time to read aloud to your child? Even if you do not have large blocks of time to devote to reading, you can make the most of every free moment. For example, utilize waiting times at the doctor or dentist. You can read to your child almost anywhere — in the car on trips, in the bed during seiges of chicken pox or other illness.

For one family in California the favorite read-aloud place is the kitchen. Dad has to be away some evenings, but when he is home, he always does the dishes after dinner, so the children can pull up chairs around Mom who sits at the table and reads aloud to the whole family.

Reading together fosters family closeness, and time spent giving "focused-attention" reading to the child at bedtime produces benefits for the relationship, whatever the age. Reading aloud is equally important for older children. Besides meeting their personal needs, it helps them continue to enjoy books for *entertainment*, so they won't automatically associate reading with workbooks, drills and tests.

Independent Reading

Having time to read silently to himself is also important for your child's development. Independent reading increases reading speed, comprehension and vocabulary. Jim Trelease, a national authority on motivating children to read, suggests that a small lamp be placed by each child's bed so he or she can read for 15 minutes before falling to sleep. Letting the child know he can stay up a little extra time to read promotes his enjoyment of reading. One family has a "Silent Sustained Reading" ("SSR") time a few times each week in which they sit together and read independently. Then they take a few minutes to discuss what each person has been reading.

A Junior Great Books group is a literary discussion group led by trained volunteers for young people in second grade through high school. They read a classic independently and then meet together for a lively discussion. For more information on this group, consult your local library, or contact: Great Books Foundation, 40 East Huron Street, Chicago, Illinois 60611, tel. (312) 332-5870.

More Benefits

Reading aloud has many other side benefits. Youthful imagination is stirred. Emotional development is encouraged. The child develops empathy and compassion as he relates to the struggles and adversities of others. "If you touch the heart with one book," says Allan Bloom, University of Chicago professor and author of *The Closing of the American Mind,* "it can transform a life."[3]

Hearing good literature read aloud provides children a rich and colorful model for their language development. It lengthens their attention span and helps them learn to follow directions better. Mysteriously, teachers report that a steady diet of good literature, read aloud at home, also improves students' attitudes toward school.

Reading is also an important foundation for good writing skills. Spending twenty minutes a day reading aloud to our children is an important step toward attainment of our goal that they learn to read, write and speak to their full potential.

Anti-TV Strategies

Researchers tell us that half of all fifth-graders spend only four minutes a day reading at home. Yet these same children spend an average of 130 minutes a day watching television. Thus it is not insignificant that it is during the fifth grade that students' scores on reading tests begin to decline rapidly.

Just as reading aloud multiplies a child's learning, a steady diet of television nullifies it. The average child between the age of two and eleven spends more than 27 hours a week watching TV, and only a small percentage of that time is spent watching educational programing.

We need to develop a strategy for dealing with television viewing in our homes and make a conscious effort to reduce the part it plays in our family lifestyle. Why? Besides the low quality of morals portrayed on many shows, television watching is destructive to a child's developing skills. Prolonged viewing produces a shortened attention span and a decrease in reading comprehension. During his watching time, the child is not interacting with others, not helping anyone, not running or playing.

Further, television watching stunts the imagination. Since everything is portrayed visually for him, the child is not required to develop the ability to form mental pictures of the action, setting and characters — as he would be if he were reading. I have found that the young person who can't picture the characters and action from the written word is handicapped when he has more lengthy, advanced reading to do. Television asks few questions, so the critical thinking skills the child will need in high school and college are stunted. Television has been called the "Great American Baby-sitter"; but with all its negative effects, it is too high a price to pay for babysitting!

Since too much television viewing handicaps learning, what can we do to limit it? We can provide many appealing alternatives, such as family projects, games, sports, art, entertaining of friends or relatives, bike riding. In this way children become participants in life, rather than mere spectators. Life is too short to spend it in front of the television set, and our children's growing and learning years are too precious to waste.

One way we can control the harmful effects of television is by turning it off completely during the school week. (This definitely aids concentration on homework.) We can limit TV viewing to the weekend, and then only in moderation. Be aware of TV reforms. I have found that both parents must be in unity in order to change any family habit, so find a way to limit television viewing that is compatible with your family. Take at least one step in the right direction. Allow your child to pick out one show a week to watch on a school night. Or, you may want to pop some popcorn and sit down together, as a family, to watch a historical special, such as a miniseries on the life of George Washington or Abraham Lincoln, with discussion afterward.

Marie Winn's book, *Unplugging the Plug-In Drug: Help Your Children Kick the TV Habit,*[4] is a step-by-step guide for organizing a week without television. It could be a helpful tool for you to use in your family situation.

When you do cut down on TV time, you will find that there is ample time in the evenings for completing homework assignments, playing games, working together on a puzzle or family project, talking, reading, and, most of all, enjoying time together free from the hectic schedules which plague most families today. It does take effort and planning to turn off the television set, but the benefits of shared experiences create a family environment in which learning can flourish.

What about the Reluctant Reader?

What about the young person who really doesn't like to read, refuses to read, or reads so slowly he doesn't enjoy books on his level? Carole Ashmore, a reading teacher from Oklahoma City, suggests several ways to motivate the reluctant reader:

- Anything we do for fun has to be relatively easy; not a task. So have available beautifully written books with good illustrations, a year or two below the child's reading level. (At the school library, often there is pressure to pick out harder books.) Reading is like riding a bike; skill progresses if the child feels comfortable and secure, not under constant pressure to perform. With easier materials, he can increase his reading speed and proficiency. Best of all, since he is out of the stressful situation of the classroom environment, his attitude improves as his reading becomes less grueling and more enjoyable.

- Many times the reluctant reader can be encouraged by having him watch a movie, such as "Black Beauty," before he reads the story in book form. When a group of school children watched programs such as George Washington, Raising the Titanic, or the National Geographic specials, all the books on those subjects quickly disappeared from the school library. When

"Anne of Green Gables" was shown, new copies of the book had to be ordered to meet the increased demand.

- Set realistic time limits for reading. Often the reluctant reader's muscle development doesn't allow for prolonged reading sessions. The typical first-grader has an attention span of about twenty minutes. This gradually increases as the child gets older.

- Parents can keep on hand a pull-out copy of the Drama in Real Life section of *Reader's Digest*. With about a sixth-grade reading ability, and a very high interest, even the reluctant reader will be able to pick the story up and become engrossed in it. Titles such as "From the Jaws of Death," "The Starduster's Last Flight," and "Rescue in Mid-air!" hook the interest of young people. Children also enjoy reading "My Most Unforgettable Moment," as well as stories about babies, older children and animals.

- Having the reluctant reader listen to a taped version of the reading material while following along silently in the book is a good way to improve his reading skills.

- Computer reading games are great for the math-oriented child who won't read. He is challenged by the mechanical aspect of the computer, but gains important reading practice.

Additional Reading

Bruce Baron, Christine Baron, Bonnie MacDonald. *What Did You Learn in School Today?* New York: Warner Books, Inc., 1983.

Gladys Hunt. *Honey for a Child's Heart*. Grand Rapids: Zondervan, 1974.

Jim Trelease. *The Read-Aloud Handbook*. New York: Penguin Books, 1986.

Marie Winn. *Unplugging the Plug-in Drug: Help Your Children Kick the TV Habit*. New York: Viking Press, 1987.

Footnotes

[1]*What Works: Research About Teaching and Learning*, United States Department of Education, William J. Bennett, Secretary, 1986, p. 15.

[2]Available from International Reading Association, 800 Barksdale Road, P. O. Box 8139, Newark, Delaware 19711.

[3]*U.S. News & World Report* (Sept. 28, 1987).

[4]Marie Winn, *Unplugging the Plug-In Drug: Help Your Children Kick the TV Habit* (New York: Viking Press, 1987).

Chapter 7

HELP YOUR CHILD BECOME A LIFELONG WRITER

"Children's ability to talk, listen, read, and write will have a lifelong effect on their ability to learn. In turn, parents have a profound influence on the development of these skills during the preschool years and beyond."

Donald Graves and Virginia Stuart

Write From the Start[1]

Why All This Fuss About Writing?

Writing is not just another subject taught in school. There is a strong relationship between writing and thinking. Thus a child's ability to write well affects his level of learning and achievement in *every* subject.

When it comes to writing, most students have difficulty organizing their thoughts coherently, so researchers tell us. A student may have bright ideas, but without skill in writing, his compositions and his answers on written exams will be confusing and disorderly. Many times his ideas will be conveyed in a garbled style so that much of their meaning is lost in transition from his fertile mind to the written page. This type of student, though he may actually be quite intelligent, is often labeled lazy or stupid, and may just barely pass from one grade level to the next.

Why encourage the development of your child's writing skills? Because, if he becomes a good, clear writer, *he will be a more successful student in every subject.* He will enjoy self-expression, be more self-reliant, and enjoy learning more — from first grade all the way through college, indeed throughout his entire life.

Stages of Writing Skill Development

Although children mature according to their own time clocks, we know that when given the time, encouragement and materials to write, the normal student will progress through certain developmental stages:

Preschool:

Basic language patterns are forming and the child is constantly building vocabulary. Drawing and scribbling are important pre-writing activities that express ideas, develop coordination and fine motor skills. The child dictates stories orally.

Kindergarten and first grade:

In this age of play, the child tends to write in the same way he plays blocks: for the sake of the activity, rather than for the final product. He rehearses by drawing and talking. He usually uses invented spelling (in which letter names represent sounds), and can often produce delightful poems, plays and stories.

Second and third grades:

At this age the child usually becomes a more fluent writer. Because of an increasing sense of audience and a desire to get things "right," he begins to move toward more conventional spelling and editing by grade three. He writes letters, stories with a plot, sequence and dialogue, and for a variety of practical reasons.

Grades four through six:

Vocabulary continues to build so that by fifth grade, the child can usually spell most of the words used in writing. He revises for better meaning and mechanics. He writes stories several pages long with conflict, characterization and dialogue. He learns to take notes, to use reference materials, the dictionary and thesaurus, and to write factual stories.

Grades seven through nine:

The typical junior high writer organizes and composes essays, stories and reports. Writing flows more easily, the student's vocabulary is wider, and he is more descriptive. Learning to edit and revise his first draft into a polished final copy will hopefully become a normal part of his writing process.

Grades ten through twelve:

The high school student gains practice in writing well-organized expository papers, the *precis*, descriptive essays and narrative essays. He learns to write a research paper using library resources. In the process, he takes notes, outlines, footnotes references and makes a bibliography. By the end of high school, his writing skills should be solid and competent.

Writing and Thinking

In our rapidly changing world, much of what our children learn in school will be obsolete in a few years. Teachers cannot provide the total information our children will need for all the problems and situations they will face in the future. So they need, most of all, to learn how to read, write and *think*. More than any other activity, writing (a focused activity which at the same time involves the hand, eye and brain) leads to clear, organized and coherent thought. Writing helps children develop vital thinking skills.

The Need for Good Writers

Writing, however, is not just for the classroom. As Kay Bishop told her freshman composition students, throughout our country there are 20 million jobs now in which people shuffle information: engineers drafting proposals, nurses and emergency medical technicians writing reports, lawyers preparing briefs, social workers filing case studies. There are memos for the boss, news stories, television scripts, poems, plays and reports on experiments. There are political campaign speeches, fund-raising and advertising copy, job resumes and letters of complaint that need to be written. We are an information community, and we need all the good, creative writers we can get.[2]

The person who can communicate effectively in speech and writing can exercise a real influence on his profession and community.

The Writing Crisis

The 1986 "Writing Report Card,"[3] a national survey of writing samples from over 55,000 students, revealed that *only 20 per cent of American students write at an adequate level.*

In addition, the national writing tests showed that:

- Fewer than one-fourth of all students can write a letter to their principals offering adequate reasons for changing a school rule.

- Barely half of eighth and eleventh graders can write a satisfactory report of a news event after being given the facts.

- Three-fourths of students say an ability to write isn't necessary to get a job.

- Almost half of the students would never write if not required to for school.

The "Writing Report Card" results puzzled educators. For although millions of dollars have been pumped into school writing programs, many students *still* can't write. Schools are making efforts to increase the frequency of writing assignments, and have begun to require that students "write across the curriculum" (that is, write in all subjects — not just in English class). Teachers are being provided the most current research information and are being encouraged to write more themselves. In addition, as a result of outstanding university projects, hundreds of teachers have been able to go out and teach writing to their colleagues and students.

However, the National Assessment of Education Progress report stated that thus far changes have had little effect on student writing. Their findings show that the most important, and the most deficient ingredient in writing skill development is the *home environment*. Too much television and too little reading and writing at home, educators say, hurt reform efforts at school.

Children who don't write at home simply don't see the value of writing at school.

Our children will become fluent, lifelong writers when we provide them four basic keys at home: *role models, resources, reasons,* and *reinforcement/encouragement* to write.

The Alcott Family: A Study in Seeds

Once there was a New England family who had great difficulty making ends meet, and often had little to eat. The father, though he tried many times to provide for his family of six, failed, and was often unemployed. The family moved twenty-nine times in twenty-eight years, usually due to lack of funds.

Yet one of the daughters of that family, Louisa Mae Alcott, grew up to become one of America's greatest writers. What did this impoverished family provide Louisa that made it possible for her to succeed so admirably in life?

Although the Alcott family was often financially deprived, they were rich in the resources necessary to encourage and stimulate a young mind: spirited daily conversation, fields and gardens to run in, family storytelling, and a few good books. Among these literary treasures were the father's beloved *Pilgrim's Progress* and the Bible, which, along with other works as could be borrowed, were often read aloud to the entire family. Sometimes a neighbor's library provided a rich supplement of books for Louisa's agile and inquisitive mind.

In addition, letters were written and exchanged with friends and relatives. For entertainment, Louisa wrote plays which she and her sisters acted out before a delighted audience of family and neighbors. Not least of all, Louisa's mother always encouraged her gifted daughter to keep a journal.[4]

Your child and mine may not grow up to be a professional writer, as Louisa Mae Alcott did, but we can provide the same rich array of resources and opportunities in our homes which will encourage our children to learn to communicate clearly in speech and writing throughout life. Whatever their vocation — engineering, law, nursing, homemaking, carpentry, or business — our children *can* write well. In the next two chapters, we will look at the seeds of a lifelong writer which we can plant in our children's lives (*role models* and *resources*) and at the ways we can water those seeds (*reasons* and *reinforcement/encouragement*).

Footnotes

[1]Donald Graves and Virginia Stuart, *Write From the Start: Tapping Your Child's Natural Writing*

Ability (New York: E.P. Dutton, 1985), p. 193.

[2]Excerpted from a talk by Kay Bishop.

[3]"Writing Report Card," National Assessment of Educational Progress, Educational Testing Services, Princeton, N J, 1986.

[4]Cornelia Meigs, *Invincible Louisa* (New York: Little, Brown and Company, 1933).

Chapter 8

SEEDS OF A LIFELONG WRITER: ROLE MODELS AND RESOURCES

Parents as Role Models

> Children need models more than critics.

Mary sat at the kitchen table, writing her weekly grocery list and figuring her checkbook balance. She addressed an envelope to mail a letter to her sister in Iowa. Five-year-old Sarah sat quietly next to her mother, busy with her own "writing" projects. In invented spelling she wrote a list of food for a tea party and drew pictures of what her dolls needed.

Just as we help our children by showing them how to make a bed, set the table, throw a baseball, or ride a bicycle, so we can show them how to write by writing — in a natural, unstressful way — as we go about our ordinary business at home.

Parents who write demonstrate that writing has value. Their children see that writing is a normal, worthwhile way to spend time. When our children observe us writing a letter to the editor of the local newspaper or to our congressman about an important issue, they see that writing serves a useful purpose in our everyday lives.

At the same time, we parents show our children the process we go through to produce that writing — making a mistake, sometimes crossing out lines, correcting words, or even throwing away our first draft and starting again. They begin to realize that writing is a process, something they don't have to "get right" the first time they try it. When we read a letter aloud, ask "How does this sound?" or discuss a newspaper article, our young people are shown that reading and writing are meant to be shared.

So the next time you write a letter, a thank-you note, or even a complaint to the telephone company, don't hide at your bedroom desk. Let your child see you writing. (Helpful Hint: Keep a pencil and paper handy so your child can do his own "writing work" along with you. Depending on his age, he can write his own "letter," draw, or make a list of his favorite stuffed animals or jobs he needs to do.)

When you make a shopping list, give your child an opportunity to make his own list. He can then see that writing is a part of everyday life. Research has proven that this "writing alongside' works much better than trying to teach a child to write by requiring him to do exercises in a workbook.

Another way to model the value of writing is to share what you write with your child. Every year at Valentine's Day, I write a poem to my husband and one to our children: Justin, Chris and Alison. In the poems I try to capture who they are and where each one is in life, to describe the joy he or she brings to me and the family, and to express my love and blessing — besides conveying a touch of humor. I read these at our Valentine family breakfast or dinner, and then present them with a little gift on a red heart.

I also write get-well poems, notes and messages to give to the members of my family. Sometimes I just write to them for fun and to express my affection for them. My children have seen me keeping a journal over the years, in addition to carrying on my personal correspondence with out-of-town friends and relatives. So they have grown up thinking of writing as a regular part of life, not just as something they have to do at school. And, as a result, their attitude toward school writing is generally positive and reflects an "I can do it" feeling.

Love Notes and Lunch Pails:

Our attitude toward writing filters through to our children. Hopefully, they do not perceive all writing as a serious, dreaded "task" or a tiring, loathsome "duty" which must be performed. To help him realize that letter writing can actually be enjoyable, try writing notes to your child purely to share an interesting or amusing anecdote or experience (such as the fact that "a funny thing happened to me on my way to work today"). These "letters" can be hidden in unexpected places so the child will find them during the course of his day — in his lunch box, under her pillow. Soon you will probably begin getting messages back.

Dr. Margaret Loeffler, Director of the Primary Division of Casady School in Oklahoma City, says that one of the best things parents of pupils in their school do is leave notes to their children in their lunch boxes. Even if the children are too young to read very well, they work out what the message says. "It amazes me how they can figure out a note if it's something Mother wrote: 'I love you'; 'Have a good day.' " These are simple things, but essential in giving children a motivation and purpose to write.

We leave our children practical messages like, "Don't forget to clean your room," and encouraging words like, "Good luck on your science test!"

We write off for information on herbs, home computers, book clubs, or whatever else we are currently interested in. Our children are thus made aware that special interests, whether tennis, ham radio, sailing, or gardening, are worth reading and writing about.

In the course of our normal, everyday routines, we parents have a unique opportunity to foster this "writing as lifestyle" attitude, as we model writing as a natural, useful and *enjoyable* activity.

Resources for Writing

If our children are to write at home, they need *resources*. And, as we have already noted, the most vital resource for writing is *reading*.

A diversity of reading materials and opportunities at home encourages our children to become lifelong writers. Children can teach themselves a great deal, if the proper reading resources are available to them. We set the stage for learning by making our homes rich educational environments.

Two daily activities to sharpen language skill development are *listening* to stories and books read aloud, and *family discussion*.

Hearing good literature read aloud expands the child's store of word meanings, sharpens his perception of correct phrasing, introduces him to varying writing styles, and increases his textual comprehension. Moreover, there is a strong correlation between listening, thinking, reading and writing. (Chapter 4 contains many ideas on how to make reading a regular part of your family's lifestyle.)

Frequent conversation is also a vital language resource. "Parents and teachers need to engage children in thoughtful discussions on all subjects — current events, nature, sports, hobbies, machines, family life, and emotions," say researchers in *What Works*.[1] In family discussions, children learn to give reasons for their opinions, discuss alternatives to problems, express their feelings, and think more clearly. Conversing with our children about the world around them gives them a great foundation in speaking and listening, an invaluable resource for the development of writing skills.

We can ask our children to describe an event or person from their day. We can encourage their observations and feelings.

A relaxed time for sharing ideas needs to be built into our daily routine. In the evening around the family dinner table seems to be the best time for our family. As we eat together with the children, my husband often asks them, "What is the most interesting thing you did, learned or saw today?" His question has opened up some lively discussions and elicited some interesting stories!

One family of early-birds had their conversation time at breakfast. Everyone got up early to share together before going off to work or school.

Family conversation can also be on a one-to-one basis. For one mother I know, the best time to talk and listen is at bedtime. She regularly takes a few minutes to sit on the side of the bed of each of her children (including teenagers) and talk, ask questions and listen.

A walk around the block can provide a sharing time. Some of the best conversations can take place as our children are working alongside us, raking leaves, doing dishes, or cooking.

"Tell It Like It Is" cards from the Ungame are also great conversation starters for long car trips or at the dinner table. Each member of the family takes a card and then shares his answer to questions like, "What kind of trophy would you like to win?" "What's your pet peeve?" or "What are three things you are thankful for?"

Materials for Drawing and Writing:

> "Children who are encouraged to draw and scribble 'stories' at an early age will later learn to compose more easily, more effectively, and with greater confidence than children who do not have this encouragement."
>
> *What Works*[2]

Next to encouraging reading and conversation in the home, one of the best things you can do for your child's writing development is to *provide accessible materials for drawing:* crayons, colored pencils, writing pencils, paper for drawing, blackboard and chalk, magic markers and paint.

Most early readers and good writers had early access to writing materials at home, and did lots of drawing. "Studies of very young children show that their carefully formed scrawls have meaning to them, and that this writing actually helps them develop language skills." (*What Works*)[3] Even before they are old enough to learn to read and write, toddlers draw and scribble messages that are filled with ideas and creativity.

Plastic or metal letters on a felt or magnetic board or the refrigerator are useful for preschoolers. Chalkboards are great language resources. Some young children like to write on toy typewriters; others like to dictate stories to Mom, who writes them down and reads them back. Dictating a story into a tape recorder is fun for some children. A little later, a typewriter or word processor is an invaluable aid to the developing young writer.

Dramatic Play: A Writing Resource:

Costumes and props are really important resources to trigger children's dramatic play, provide language practice, and at the same time help children find a great usefulness for writing. Besides being purely entertainment, it gives them a reason to read and write when they're little. They imitate Mom and Dad and big sister or brother.

Dramatic play motivates children to want to learn to read and write. So pencils and paper can be placed near their other toys. Then they can write as a part of their imaginative play — while playing nurse, restaurant, or store. For example, when they play office, they can write letters, address them, and then "mail" them in their own make-believe mailbox.

Sometimes children like to make labels for their toys and signs for their rooms: "Sara Jane Bear." "Keep out!" "Boys/Girls only!"

Freeda Richardson, a creative writing teacher I know, says that the favorite dramatic play of her daughter Laura is "store." Freeda got her a receipt book at the office supply house and an old adding machine from the pawnshop. An antique telephone mounted on the wall completed the props, and the "store" has generated many hours of creative play and writing: orders, receipts, lists of returned merchandise, and other "business" records.

For several years my daughter, Alison, enjoyed playing hospital and making short medical reports on clipboard paper about each of her doll "patients." She also set up a school and an office for which she carried on correspondence and listed employees. Such writing, done in the context of fantasy play, is an important part of growing and learning.

A large chalkboard is a good tool for playing school, practicing the alphabet or writing notes. Freeda says that she bought Laura a large chalkboard for her room when the child was only four years old. "We leave each other messages on the board. When she has a friend spend the night, they leave her a 'THANK YOU' on the chalkboard. This summer I had to be at the university many days, and Laura became bored and asked, 'What can I do tomorrow?' I wrote on her chalkboard a list of activities that might be fun."

Word Games:

Another source for writing is word games. They can be played just about anywhere: in the car, at the doctor's office, in the kitchen. Word games foster language skills and build vocabulary.

Try a word game like, "I'm thinking of something that starts with a 'D.' " Or, "Who am I?" (give characteristics of an object or person, and let the child guess the correct answer). Crossword puzzles, anagrams and cryptograms are all fun. On a long trip, we always work a big crossword puzzle together as a family (five heads are better than one). Making up rhymes, limericks, and tongue-twisters is good language play. Also amusing, as well as educational, are games like "Opposites" (you give the word *hot* and your child has to supply the opposite) or "Categories" (in which you take turns naming all the fruits or brands of cars you can think of).

You can purchase and play commercially prepared word games like ABC, Scrabble, Scrabble Junior, Password or Perquakey — super vocabulary builders! Charades (pantomiming words — or book and movie titles, in the case of older children) is a real favorite of most youngsters because it involves action.

All of these resources provide a rich background for your developing writer.

Footnotes

[1] *What Works: Research About Teaching and Learning,* United States Department of Education, William J. Bennett, Secretary, 1986, p. 15.

[2] Ibid., p. 14.

[3] Ibid.

Chapter 9

WATERING THE SEEDS: REASONS AND ENCOURAGEMENT TO WRITE

Reasons:
Motivation for Writers

Writing doesn't need to be a boring subject. With a little creativity, parents can help their children discover that writing can be as much fun as drawing, singing or making puppets.

The more writing your child does at home, the better writer he will be. And we know that children will write if we give them good, practical reasons to do so. Here are several activities you can suggest to your child. They will water the seeds of a lifelong writer which you have planted in him and will activate those seeds to bloom into language fluency. Pick the suggestions and ideas best suited to your child's age, personality and stage of development.

- Have your child make place cards for special family dinners. Alison considers this her job. She likes to decorate the place cards with a little picture or sticker when she sets the table for Christmas, Easter, birthdays or other special occasions.

- Help your child make an "All About Me" scrapbook. Let him choose 10 to 15 pictures of himself taken from infancy to the present and place them in chronological order. Then he can tape or glue the pictures in a scrapbook or on folder pages. He can write, or dicate for you to write, a caption to go underneath each photo.

- Have your child make lists: grocery lists, lists of what he will need to complete his science project, birthday lists, lists of things he will need for his weekend camping trip, lists of friends to invite to a party, lists of his homework assignments and daily chores.

- Have your child make maps and write directions: to a friend's house, to church, to school, for your next trip. Write directions for things he knows how to do, like making a birdhouse, planting and growing a flower from a seed, or how to prepare his favorite dish.

- Have your child organize a treasure hunt. This is Nicholas Bishop's favorite indoor game. He makes a whole string of clues, written on slips of paper, for his cousin to follow: "Your next clue is found in the living room by something green." "Now look under the bed." "Beside the dog's bed is your treat." Then he plants a package of gum or a box of raisins at the end of the treasure hunt.

(One mother used to meet her son at the door every day at noon with a "treasure hunt" clue in her hand. At the end of the hunt was his lunch. This game was not only "rewarding," it also encouraged the boy to learn to think through the clues in logical order — and now he has a real gift for sequential reasoning.)

This is a good example of how playing and writing mixed together can make for an enjoyable hour of indoor fun and learning.

- Have your child make original birthday, Valentine's Day and Christmas cards, writing his own greeting or verse in each one. Have him create his own original birthday party invitations, decorate them with colorful stickers and address the envelopes in his very own handwriting (or printing).

- Suggest that your child write a script for a puppet show and perform it on a rainy day.

- Have your child write his own menu and play "restaurant."

- Have your child put together a family newsletter, with each member of the family contributing stories or recent happenings, funny sayings, cartoons and illustrations. Help him make photocopies of the letter and send it out to all the extended family each season.

- Subscribe to a writing magazine for your child and suggest that he submit poems and stories to it. Two creative writing magazines for children are: *Shoe Tree*, P.O. Box 452, Belvedere, N J 07823, and *Stone Soup*, published by Children's Art Foundation, P.O. Box 83, Santa Cruz, CA 95063. These periodicals publish book reviews, poems, stories and pictures by youngsters.

Encourage Story Writing and Book Making:

Even young children can write stories. Early childhood educator, Maria Montessori, advocated teaching children to write before they learn to read. You can encourage this development by recording the stories and experiences your child shares with you.

Have the child dictate a story as you write it down. He may want to dictate his own version of Red Riding Hood or The Three Bears. In dictating, he learns that his ideas can be put down on paper with symbols (words). He begins to understand what writing is, and this understanding sparks his interest in expressing himself on paper. Read your child's story back to him just as he dictated it.

Soon he will want to do the writing himself. You can help him make his own books, with pictures and homemade bindings.

Diana Purser, a high school English teacher in Zwibrupcken High School, located on an American air base in Germany, says that the best thing she ever did to encourage her little girl's writing was to make a book of her story.

"When April was about four years old we did our first 'book' together. It was three pieces of typing paper, trimmed and stapled. April dictated a story to me about a princess in a castle. She drew and colored some pictures to go with the story. It was a small book, but a great beginning! April loved it, and we still have it in her baby book. She has done other books, but that first one remains the favorite."

If children are encouraged, they will write, very early, from age four and a half. Writing experts tell us not to criticize spelling and punctuation in these early writing efforts. The children will be using "invented spelling," which means that, since they don't yet know the conventional spelling, they will be writing words down as they hear them. "Children are very sensitive to not wanting to be wrong," says Dr. Loeffler, "and if parents continually correct invented spelling, children stop writing."

There is a great deal of evidence to indicate that when children invent spelling, they don't even necessarily spell words the same way twice. So parents don't have to worry that a mistake in spelling made by their five- or six-year-old will be forever ingrained in the child's mind if they allow it to go uncorrected. At this stage, children's writing is much like their drawing, simply a means of self-expression. As they begin to read more, gradually they will begin to incorporate conventional spelling into their writing. Spelling is a developmental skill. By fourth or fifth grade, children have learned how to spell most of the words they need to express their ideas in writing, so they soon learn to edit and revise their own work.

Encourage your child to read his writing aloud, so he will develop a sense of audience. This is the first step in learning to revise. He will learn to revise *if* he sees a need for revision: Does the writing communicate what he wants it to say to someone?

At the early preschool and elementary stages, allow your child to enjoy writing, appreciate his efforts, and concentrate on the meaning he is trying to express. (We will discuss editing skills in Chapter 12.)

Letter Writing:

Letter writing provides one of the best reasons to write. Correspondence with out-of-town family members or friends is great practice in practical writing (especially if the person writes back!).

Since they live in Germany where she teaches school at Zwibrupcken, Diana Purser says she and her family write letters to family and friends in the United States, because overseas phone calls are so expensive. As a result, her daughter, April, aged seven, has done lots of letter writing too. She began with a rebus letter, composed before she could write the entire alphabet. It looked like this:

Granma: Thank you for the 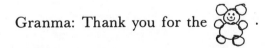 .

My friend, Nicholas Bishop, who is also seven, likes to send get-well cards to teachers and friends.

Freeda Richardson encourages her children to help her clip little humorous pieces from *Reader's Digest*, newspaper cartoons, or quotes that would be encouraging to Grandpa, aunts and uncles or other family members to whom they write. She and the children send the clippings along with their letters. Now her children have begun to find their own clippings and quotes to send with their letters.

Our son, Justin, writes letters to friends in Pennsylvania, Hawaii and Minnesota. Alison writes to friends in New Mexico and Texas. Since we recently moved to Maine, we all write to friends and relatives back home in Oklahoma.

Vivian Nida's first-grade son, Hunter, found a "fun reason" to write letters: his Nintendo television video game. As Vivian says: "At my class reunion this summer, Hunter met a little boy from Indiana who also had a Nintendo. At the end of the game you rescue the princess. Hunter had been trying and trying to rescue her, but in order to get to the castle where the princess is held captive, you have to collect extra men along the way. The little boy he met, Ben, said, 'I know where there's an extra man on the screen.' Hunter said, 'Where is it?' The boy tried to explain but said, 'When I get home I'll draw what the screen looks like, and I'll send you the picture and explain.' "

Vivian says that when Hunter got the boy's letter in the mail, he and his sister Brooke, 10, were both excited. They could hardly wait to get to the screen. With Ben's directions, they found the extra man, and saved the princess for the first time. Now they are looking at the game trying to find other hidden things, drawing them on paper to send to Ben. It provides a "fun reason" to correspond in letters, and a real purpose for them to write.

Pen Pals:

Communicating with a pen pal across the country or the globe also provides a good reason to write. Through a lively correspondence with a pen pal, your child gains insight into how people in other cultures live. You can request a pen pal for your child by sending a self-addressed, stamped envelope to:

International Friendship League
Department A
22 Batterymarch
Boston, MA 92109

World Pen Pals
1690 Como Avenue
St. Paul, MN 55108

Student Letter Exchange
R.F.D. - 4
Waseca, MN 56093

Journals:

A journal is a record of ideas and thoughts kept in a book reserved for that purpose. Let your child pick one out — cloth, spiral or any type of notebook. Encourage him to choose a title for his journal: "Jimmy's Jottings," "Sara's Slices of Life." Whereas a diary lists daily events, a journal is more of an idea bank, a resource and practice book. Here are some of the things your child can keep in a journal:

- His favorite sayings, scripture verses, poems, messages on churches' signs and bumper stickers

- A list of ideas for projects he would like to do, places he would like to visit

- A record of a dialogue he heard today

- A record of insights he received today

- Highlights of a trip he took

- Pencil or pen sketches

- The description of a favorite person

- A narration of an event that surprised, frustrated, delighted or angered him

- A record of his hopes, plans and dreams
- A record of questions he has about anything
- Poems, stories and prayers
- His opinion of a movie he saw or a book he read

Some children naturally like to keep journals, while others need some encouragement. On our trip to Washington, DC and Maine this past summer, I decided to give travel journals a try. I got each of the children a cloth-bound blank book, and told them I wanted them to write the highights of each day's travel. With a 4,000-mile journey ahead, I figured they would have plenty of time to write. So with a few groans, they began.

These travel journals had some success, and I learned some things in the process (which I share with you in the form of suggestions):

1. Offer an incentive — even a small one like sugarless gum or a Tootsie-Roll Pop — to your child if he has finished his journal writing at the end of each day.

2. Encourage your child to keep up with his writing daily, even if he only writes for five minutes. He will get bogged down and discouraged if he has three of four days to "catch up on."

3. Keep the journal *accessible*, not under mounds of suitcases in the back of the car where it will be difficult to locate.

4. Encourage your child to write only the *most special, favorite* things he did that day — highlights only! This is not a diary listing every meal and activity of each day. Recording all that detail overwhelms children, especially if the family visits a lot of places. Instead, have your child describe the most unusual exhibit at the museum or his favorite animal at the zoo. If this concept is understood from the beginning, travel journaling will be much more workable and enjoyable.

A record of the trip written from the child's own perspective will be great to look back to and remember. He can illustrate it with pencil sketches, or tuck in photographs.

Here are some excerpts from our travel journals, summer 1987 (reproduced with permission of their young authors):

"Today I went to the Smithsonian Natural History Museum and saw the dinosaurs. I was able to get a wheelchair and Justin wheeled me around. It was fun but a lot of people stared at me."

Chris, age 13

(He had just had an emergency appendectomy less than a week before we left home and couldn't walk far enough to see everything: hence the wheelchair.)

"Everywhere you look in Virginia, a picture could be painted — the rolling green valleys, masses of roadside trees, perfectly planted rows of corn. The other night we went to Alexandria, Old Town. It was very picturesque — the jointed townhouses, little knick-knack shops. There was lots of activity: crowds, lights, noise, cars and street people."

Justin, age 16

"On Lake Pennesseewassee in Norway, Maine, I learned to water ski. It was my favorite thing. I tried three times before I got up and went the whole way around the lake on skis. The water was freezing. The lake was wavy because of the wind. It felt unbelievable when I got up on the water skis!"

Alison, age 10

After the trip, encourage your child to continue journal writing: about the first day of school; about experiences at home and school; about people, goals, ideas. Journaling is excellent writing practice.

Logs for Learning:

A log is a very practical learning tool for students of any age. Logs particularly appeal to the science/math-oriented child. He keeps an on-going record of what he is learning as it takes place, thus encouraging both his thinking and writing skills. In his own style and language, your child can take notes on a nature walk and write a log of the autumn things he sees and collects. An older student can record the methods and results of his rocket experiment. Another child may keep a log of the weather over a certain period of time.

In his log, the child can:

- describe problems

- note discoveries

- clarify concepts

- record ideas for future projects

Notes, Notes, Notes:

Notes are a particular reason to write at home. Each member of the family can be encouraged to communicate with notes: "Please feed the dog and cat!" "Have a good day!" "God loves you!" "Welcome home, Dad!"

Keep a bulletin board for reminders about chores, to express praise and appreciation, to leave holiday messages or to give encouragement for a difficult test or soccer game. Some families use a big white chalkless board. Others use sticky-back "post it" pads to leave notes on mirrors, pillows and just about anywhere.

You can mount a letter box or basket on your child's door to receive messages and letters. In the kitchen you can have a letter box for notes from your family to you.

Encouragement: Reinforcement for Writers

When our children do write, they need our praise and affirmation, not criticism. One way to show that we value written expression is to keep a *folder* or file of our children's writing. We can display the writing on the refrigerator or bulletin board for a time, and then it goes into a file with the particular child's name on it, and the year in which it was written (Alison's Writing — 1987). At the end of the year, this writing file is saved along with other important keepsakes. Then we start a new file of writing. At any time, the children can get out the previous year's files and see what they wrote that year.

We can respond as sensitive, attentive readers to the ideas our children express in writing. We can focus on content. Encourage your child to read his writing aloud. Be aware of his feelings, and ask questions such as, "Can you tell me more about this story?" "What's going to happen next?" "How did you find out about this?" Take a positive approach and always find something good to say about what he has written.

When children share their writing with me, I often have to tie my invisible English teacher's "red pen hand" behind my back; otherwise, I will be tempted to over-react to (or even try to correct!) their mistakes. I must be tactful, focusing on what they did *right* in the paper — the descriptive word used, the interesting twist at the end of the story, the neat handwriting. I must remember that writing is a *process*, and that if errors are pointed out too soon, too harshly, or too often, children won't keep trying to write. Treating their writing with respect fosters a good self-image and a sense of trust.

Given these role models, resources, reasons, and this reinforcement, your child can become a fluent writer, not just during his school years, but throughout his life.

Additional Reading

Lucy McCormick Calkins. *Lessons from a Child: On the Teaching and Learning of Writing.* Portsmouth: Heinemann Educational Books, 1983.

Donald Graves and Virginia Stuart. *Write from the Start: Tapping Your Child's Natural Writing Ability.* New York: E.P. Dutton, 1985.

Linda Leonard Lamme. *Growing Up Writing: Sharing With Your Children the Joys of Good Writing.* Washington, DC: Acropolis Books, 1984.

Frank Smith. *Essays into Literacy.* Portsmouth: Heinemann Educational Books, 1983.

Denny Taylor. *Family Literacy: Young Children Learning To Read and Write.* Portsmouth: Heinemann Educational Books, 1983.

Chapter 10

DEVELOPING MATH SKILLS

I remember all the games I played with my brothers and sisters while growing up. I watched and learned from my big sisters and proudly graduated from Go Fish and Old Maid to Hearts, Monopoly, Parcheesi and Chinese checkers. I had to really develop my skill to be allowed to play with the three "big girls." Then in turn I taught games to my little sister and brother.

Besides "Chinese School," "Simon Says," "I Spy" and "Mother May I?," the game of jacks occupied much of our spare time also. Getting "onesies" and "twosies" was easy, but the higher the numbers got, the faster my little fingers had to move. Before I even started to school, one of my goals as a five-year-old was "to get all of the pigs in the pen" and not get my "cart before the horse."

And then there was the magic of jumping rope. The myriad of jump-rope counting games kept us hopping up and down, trying to be the winner.

We didn't know that in all these play-time activities we were learning valuable math concepts like counting, sequencing, combining, sorting, logic and problem solving, but none of the six of us ever had any difficulty in math.

> "Arithmetic is where the answer is right and everything is nice and you can look out the window and see the blue sky — or the answer is wrong and you have to start all over and try it again and see how it comes out this time."
>
> Carl Sandburg
> "Arithmetic"

I have a child who loves math and another who prefers literature. One finds math easy and fun, and one sometimes struggles with the many problems assigned for homework.

As I interviewed math teachers, I asked questions like:

- "How can we build a good solid foundation for math skills with preschoolers?"

- "How can we encourage positive attitudes and avoid 'math anxiety'?"

- "What about kids and calculators?"

- "How can we enrich math learning in the middle years?"

- "How can we help when a child is 'stuck' on a difficult math problem?"

As I share the responses I received, and what I have learned as a parent journeying down "mathematics lane" with my own children these past ten years, I hope you and your child are helped to be more enthusiastic about the wonderful opportunities all around us to develop good math skills.

Role Model

If math was your worst subject in school, don't tell your child!

> "Some people say, 'I don't have a mind for math.' We know now that every person has a mind for math, provided the math is presented in an understandable manner. Research has shown that children of all ethnic backgrounds, girls as well as boys, are equally capable of learning mathematics."
>
> Claudia Zaslavsky
>
> *Preparing Young Children for Math*[1]

Math teachers agree that one of the *biggest obstacles* to a child's success in math is the attitude he brings into the classroom.

"Try to make sure," said Vicki Hamilton, a middle school math teacher in Dallas, Texas, "that you do not create an 'out' for your child by telling him, 'It's okay to do poorly in math; I wasn't good in it either.' " Telling your child "I hated math" is a sure-fire way to undermine his learning by instilling in him a negative attitude.

Instead, be positive! Be positive about the projects you do that utilize math: bookkeeping involved with your job, measuring and timing baked goods, balancing your checkbook, using coupons at the grocery store — and let your child observe and talk with you about your work.

One mother whose child accompanied her to her part-time job at a clothing store and watched her keep the books, insisted upon having her own ledger and receipt book to fill out. She spent hours writing numbers in her "office books," and acquired an early interest in math.

Be aware of the math all around you and seize opportunities to share with your child the importance of mathematics. Let him see that it is practical and relates to real life. You can point out that numbers are everywhere, that we use them constantly — often without even thinking of it. Thus numbers will make more sense to him and computing will be more natural in the classroom.

Lynn Fuller, a sixth-grade teacher in Pawhuska, Oklahoma, says that sports is a perfect way for children to see math in everyday life. She suggests that parents of sports-minded children call attention to batting averages, strategy and plays in football and the numbers on soccer, basketball and football uniforms.

She also notes that checkbooks and money are always of interest to youngsters. You can point out that measuring is important when you cook, ride a bike, build a house or sew.

Time is important to all of us. Sales reductions, speed limit signs, the distance between towns on the highway — whether in little or big ways, we're always using math.

We can also talk about all the occupations that use math, and for which math is a prerequisite:

- Computer fields
- Architecture
- Science
- Business Management
- Engineering
- Aerospace
- Medical, surgical and nursing fields

In almost any occupation, math is involved in some way. We don't drop a "math is important" lecture on our children one day and expect them to suddenly become math-oriented. Instead we share informally as we go on errands, travel, cook, work and live together, constantly demonstrating for our children the value of math skills in everyday life.

Building a Solid Foundation
for Young Children

Children learn best from hands-on activities in which they use math for real reasons in the course of their day and from play in which they build on their understanding. We know that children learn to count naturally if they have concrete things to count. Even in elementary math, they need concrete objects until they have reached a certain level of development. Children pushed too early into abstract mathematical concepts and symbols often develop "math phobia." Such children display little motivation for math, dislike it for no apparent reason, and seem to "prove" their lack of affinity for the subject by doing poorly on math tests.

"We can make math fun, more like a puzzle than a chore," says Lynn Fuller. There's no need to push your preschooler to become involved in organized math activities or to spend his time laboring over math workbooks. Instead, take advantage of informal opportunities *to incorporate math into his play time and the regular course of family life.*

Patti Milburn, a middle school math teacher in Oklahoma City, points out that even as early as his infancy, you can begin to introduce your child to math by counting aloud his fingers and toes, by singing nursery rhymes and songs which involve counting and by counting the buttons on his sweater while dressing him.

Here are some ways teachers suggest to build a solid foundation for young children (these suggestions apply to children from *preschool through age 8*):

Sorting:	Let your child sort laundry, blocks, and money (into stacks of quarters, dimes, nickels, and pennies). He can sort silverware, putting away knives, forks and spoons in their proper slots. (Good practice in categorizing.)
Setting the table:	(Learning a pattern is foundational to math skills.) "Let's count how many of us will be here tonight for dinner." "Where does the fork (spoon, knife) go?"

Cooking:

Most children love to help in the kitchen and in the process they learn about measuring, temperature ("bake at 300 degrees"), time ("our muffins will be ready in 30 minutes") and dividing portions.

Telling time:

"How much longer before the Charlie Brown special?" "How long to lunch?" You need to always have at least one good-sized, clock (not digital) visible in the home.

Getting from place to place:

Count the blocks to the ice cream store or to the house of a friend or relative. If you drive, ask: "How much gas will we need to fill the tank?" "What is the speed limit?" Older children can help figure how long it would take to drive instead of fly to Grandma's in Texas.

Counting toys:

Count toys while putting them away on shelves or in bins. Count out cookies or grapes: "Here are your two cookies (grapes): one, two."

Puzzles and blocks:

Puzzles give practice in identifying shapes and matching colors. Children learn many math concepts while *playing with blocks:* weight, size, spatial relationships, order, proportion.

Reading a calendar:

"How many days until your birthday? Let's count them." An advent calendar is a "fun way" to learn about the calendar and to count off the days until the arrival of Christmas.

Comparing sizes and amounts:

"Which apple is bigger?" "How many oranges does it take to make a pound?"

Measuring height:

"Who is tallest: Dad, Mom or Sister?" Keep a board or colored tape to record your child's height.

Singing number songs and fingerplay:	"Five Frogs Sitting on a Log," "Ten Little Indians," "Five Little Pumpkins," "Ten Bears in Bed."
Reading:	Libraries are full of delightful picture books that demonstrate math concepts! Suggested books: *Arthur's Funny Money*, L. Hoban (New York: Harper & Row, 1981); *Caps for Sale*, E. Slobodkina (New York: Harper & Row, 1970); *The Tenth Good Thing about Barney*, J. Viorst (New York: Atheneum, 1971); *Building a House*, B. Barton (New York: Greenwillow, 1978).
Pretend play:	Play restaurant or store using real coins. Play space travel using a one-gallon ice cream container for rocket fuel.

Using numbers naturally when you talk about objects helps build your child's math vocabulary, says Patti Milburn. "Here are three grapes for you! Eat one. Now three take away one leaves how many? One, two!" "Do you want your cheese sandwich cut into halves or fourths?" Then demonstrate.

Parents who verbalize and interact with their children can easily incorporate math into daily life, instilling in their youngsters a positive attitude toward this vital life skill.

"Most importantly, have quality time together with your preschooler. During this time incorporate play with working with shapes, counting toys and objects, sorting and grouping objects together to show how objects can be added and taken away from each other."

Dana Smith

Middle school teacher

There are plenty of games for building math skills. A deck of playing cards offers children opportunities to: match suits and numbers, count, practice logic and problem solving, and play Concentration. (Place all the cards face down on a table in rows. Each player gets to turn over two cards. If the cards match, the player keeps them. If they do not match, they are turned face down again. When the player makes a pair, he gets to try again. The object of the game is to remember where the cards are located, make the most pairs and win the most cards. This game improves visual memory and teaches number associations.) Young children can also play simple games of Go Fish, Old Maid, Slap Jack or War (sometimes called Battle).

Child psychologist, Dr. Margie Golick, tells of a six-year-old who, after a year in kindergarten and half a year in first grade, was still unable to remember which number was which. He was easily distracted, clumsy and spatially confused. Dr. Golick taught the child to play Go Fish. After a week of playing the game, he was able to master instant recognition of the numbers 1 to 10.[2]

Dr. Golick points out that an inexpensive deck of cards is the best educational tool available to teach a child essential math concepts of: sorting and grouping; space, time and number; logic and problem solving. For the learning-disabled child, card games are particularly helpful because they motivate him "to work at something over and over again just because it is so intriguing, so challenging, or so much fun."[3]

Crazy Eights, Spades, and Hearts are great card games to play with children of elementary age or older. The game of Hearts, for instance, provides practice in these learning skills:

- categorizing

- counting

- judging quantitative rank of numbers

- considering several factors at once

- maintaining variable set

- adding (including adding negative numbers)

- reasoning

- memory

- calculating probabilities

- developing strategies

In addition, your child's math skills will be further developed by playing games such as:

- bean bag toss

- dominoes

- bowling

- board games like Chutes and Ladders, Monopoly, Clue, Battleship and Presto-Change-O

Computer games can also build skills. For example, "Master Blaster," for ages 6 through 11, provides practice in basic arithmetic facts, fractions, decimals, and percentages. "Learning about Numbers," for ages 4 through 10, includes drills with counting, as well as practice in telling time and basic math facts. "Addition Magician," for ages 8 through 10, builds speed with sums up to 18.

Memorizing Math Facts

One of the most important math skills for elementary school children is the ability to memorize addition, subtraction, multiplication and division facts. Mastery of these basic operations is *foundational and absolutely essential*. Without them the child will be handicapped in junior high school math and beyond.

" 'In our rush to teach the *whys* and *hows* of math, we've failed to teach the *whats*. And when you're trying to compute costs, mortgage interest, or gas mileage, you need to know *what*, say 6 X 9 equals. That means

"6 X 9 = 54" should be memorized,' says Beverly Schriefels, a fifth grade and gifted resource teacher in St. Francis, Minnesota."[4]

These math facts are presented at school, but for most students, there must be some help and practice at home if complete mastery is to be gained on schedule.

> "Memorizing can help students absorb and retain the factual information on which understanding and critical thought are based."
> *What Works*[5]

The daily study period at home is a good time to work on weak skills or to repeat math facts. You can make this exercise more fun by using a tape recorder and flashcards. The child reads the fact "8 − 3 = _____" and then pauses. He can go through about 10 to 15 cards, then rewind and play the tape back, supplying the correct answers.

Teachers say that memorizing is always easier with two people — child and child, parent and child, or tutor and child. Drill, practice and usage make these facts easier to retain.

Addition/Subtraction Bingo and Multiplication Bingo are games that promote math skill retention. You can quiz your child in the car — working on 2s, 3s, 5s or whichever set of multiplication facts is weakest.

Alison invented a multiplication "Mother May I?" game. I would hold up a flashcard with a math fact (such as 9 X 7) on it. If Alison got the answer right, she was allowed to take one step forward: if her answer was wrong, she had to take one step backward. We went through a whole stack of multiplication facts. When Alison had learned them well enough to advance step by step all the way to where I was sitting "at the head of the class," she received her reward — a hug and a small treat.

What About Calculators?

Math teachers agree that during the elementary school years children are still learning basic computational facts and need to develop their personal math skills before allowing a calculator to do the work for them. During regular classroom hours, and in their home study, it is best for them to do their own "calculating." Calculators have a place in math, but should be introduced only after children have mastered the basics. They can best be utilized when students begin to solve mathematical problems involving integers or formulas, patterns or sequences. Knowledge of the proper use of a calculator is essential in our electronic society, but that knowledge should come at the right stage of development.

Don L'Heureux, a teacher in Yarmouth Intermediate School in Yarmouth, Maine, says that through fourth grade math, students should not rely on a calculator to do their thinking. Learning multiplication skills teaches them many concepts such as understanding what a perfect square is. Knowing multiplication tables will save them time in doing square root, percentage, and positive and negative numbers. In trigonometry and higher level math, the calculator is a valuable tool which saves time and helps focus on higher thinking skills.

The exceptions for calculator use in elementary grades might be occasional problem-solving and challenge activities, in which the emphasis is placed on "how to do" and problem-solving skills, not on basic computation. Let your child use a calculator for fun and motivation, teachers say. Allow him to use it to check his work. But if he finds that an answer is wrong, he should rework the problem himself before using the calculator to recheck it.

Enrichment for the Middle School Years

1. Estimating is a valuable practical skill for children to learn math. 'When students can make good estimates of the answer to an arithmetic problem, it shows they understand the problem. This skill leads them to reject unreasonable answers and to know whether they are 'in the ballpark.' "[6]

One way to work on estimating is with shopping skills. Patti Milburn suggests letting your child estimate the cost of the items on your grocery list by adding up the prices listed in the newspaper food ads, deducting for any coupons.

If you see a half-price sale, have the child help you figure the prices. At the grocery store, if bananas are three pounds for a dollar, ask him to figure how much it will cost to buy one pound, two pounds or five pounds.

2. Let your child have a lemonade or cookie stand, a toy sale or help you with a garage sale. He can help you price objects to be sold and act as your cashier.

3. 'Mental Math' is good exercise for children, says Shirley Pugh, elementary teacher. Ask your child a continuous problem (age-appropriate) to be figured in his head. For example: 2 plus 5 times 6 minus 7 times 3 minus 4 equals _____. Use only addition and subtraction for a first- or second-grader; and other suitable operations for an older child.

4. Setting up a budget can make math skills practical and meaningful, suggests Shirley Pugh. Have a goal (the purchase of a certain toy), find out how much money it will take to reach that goal, how much weekly allowance the child can save, and then provide ways for him to earn that amount by doing special jobs. Plot these: determine the approxiate date of the purchase, then keep daily records of funds.

5. "One of the most difficult concepts in middle school math is percentage," says Patti Milburn. Give your child practical, concrete percentage problems to figure out. One of her most successful projects is allowing her seventh-graders to design a sale circular. She gives them the items, their original price and the percentage markdown. Then they have to figure the sale price and incorporate all the necessary information into a circular ad.

6. She also suggests another very practical application of math principles — having your child measure his room (or your entire

house) and figure the square footage of the floor space, as though you were going to purchase enough carpet to cover it.

7. Use travel as a way of practicing math skills. Your child can use a map to determine how far it is to your vacation destination, then figure the amount of total transportation costs, taking into account the difference in camping fees and motel rates.

8. Math puzzles that come in paperback books are enjoyable and challenging ways to practice math skills. (Dover Publications is the best source of these puzzles.)

I'm Stuck!

Let's face it, now and then we are going to have an opportunity to coach a child through a difficult set of math problems. (Of course, they're hard; that's why they're called *problems!*) What if he gets *stuck?* What if *you* are stuck? Here are some good homework strategies for math:

- If the math assignment is long or unusually difficult, set a kitchen timer for 20 or 30 minutes and have your child work for that set period. Then at the sound of the alarm, let him take a break and come back later to finish the assignment. If the child comes home totally overwhelmed by the large number of problems he has been assigned, divide them out: have him work one-fourth of them after school, one-fourth right before dinner, one-fourth after dinner and then finish up right before bedtime.

- Patti Milburn suggests that, especially with a new lesson, you have the child do three or four of the assigned problems. Then check those and have him do eight or ten more. This prevents his doing a whole lesson wrong.

- If the child is really stuck, he needs a push, says Shirley Pugh. Don't let an obstacle become an excuse to quit. Show the child how to do a similar problem; then see if he can handle the original troublesome one.

Lynn Fuller says, "Don't just give your child the answer. Instead, ask him questions to walk him through each step of the problem." Example: "What do you think we should try first? Okay, let's make up a simpler problem and see if that will work. Good, that should work here too. Now what will we do next?" (Or, "That didn't work quite right, what other way can we try?")

If you feel one way of explaining a concept isn't working, try another way — like using manipulatives. (This helps kinesthetic learners and also any child who has trouble with abstractions.) Draw pictures or graphs (good for the visual learner) to make the problem concrete. For the auditory child, have him start at the beginning and explain to you what the teacher taught in class concerning this type problem. Listen for concept trouble or misinformation, and work the child toward understanding. Explain orally, and then turn the tables and let him teach you to do a problem.

Also, keep on hand the name and telephone number of a friend you can call for assistance. Consider sending the child in for extra help from his teacher; most teachers have time set aside before or after school to give special attention to students who need extra help. The teacher may recommend a tutor outside of school to work with the child once a week if there is a big learning gap.

Many cities now have Homework Hot-Lines for children who get stuck and have no one at home to help them. The Hot-Line is a service provided by teachers or university students who stand by to assist pupils over the phone during the usual homework hours.

• Always encourage your child's self-reliance and sense of responsibility. These are crucial to his learning!

Studying for a Math Test

Find out the day of the week on which the math test is usually given (this day is probably consistent). Don't wait until your child comes home and announces, "We're having a math test tomorrow." Keep up with what the child is studying and schedule periodic reviews so he won't feel panicked or have to "cram" just before the test. If you are in doubt about what major skills are to be mastered by the students during that school year, ask the teacher.

The best way to study for a math test is to actually rework each type of problem that will be on the exam. Problems from classwork and homework assignments during the week and from previous tests are the best sources to use as sample problems. And *be defensive*, teachers say. Make sure your child has gotten the necessary help from his teacher *before* the test.

Inequalities, proportions, algebraic solutions, commuting with integers — all these your child can tackle better if he has a strong foundation in number concepts gained by working and playing with concrete objects as a preschooler; if he has a *positive* attitude about the value of math; if he masters the math facts and basic concepts like estimating, rounding, place value, and decimals; and if he has developed good study habits and test-taking skills.

Footnotes

[1] Claudia Zaslavsky, *Preparing Young Children for Math: A Book of Games* (New York: Schocken Books, 1979), p. xii.

[2] Margie Golock, *Deal Me In: The Use of Playing Cards in Teaching and Learning* (New York: Monarch Press, Simon and Schuster, Inc., 1981), p. 22.

[3] Ibid, p. 9.

[4] "Memorization: Making It Work in Your Class," *Learning,* (Nov.-Dec. 1985).

[5] *What Works: Research About Teaching and Learning,* United States Department of Education, William J. Bennett, Secretary, 1986, p. 37.

[6] Ibid, p. 31.

Chapter 11

STUDY SKILLS:
KEY TO ACHIEVEMENT

One year Steven was in my freshman English class. He had an outstanding IQ and loved science fiction. However, instead of doing his homework, he stayed up late, sometimes until 2 a.m., playing with his computer. He had no set study hours and no schedule for sleeping. Rather than following a planned, balanced diet, he preferred stuffing himself at all hours with sugar-laden junk food. As a result of his poor eating, sleeping and study habits, he was usually drowsy and listless in class. Consequently, in spite of his high IQ, he was failing not only English, but most of his other ninth-grade courses — and becoming quite depressed about it all.

Steven is a prime example of the fact that just having a high IQ does not ensure success in school. The way children study has a major impact on how much they learn. Researchers have found that the parents of successful students take time to help their children develop effective study strategies.

Lowering the Boom

When we parents get busy with our own concerns, it is easy to become lax about our children and their study habits. Sometimes we neglect to keep in touch with their teachers, to inform ourselves about their progress in class, or to check to see if they are turning in their assigments on time. We assume that our children are "doing okay in school" — until we receive a warning slip from their teacher in the mail, or until they actually bring home a report card full of low grades!

For many years while teaching English in high school and junior high, I saw parents "lower the boom" on their children the last four or five days of the nine-week grading period, when it was almost too late to recover. "You're grounded for the next month if you don't make a C in English!" they would say in frustration, instead of supporting their student's learning and insisting on good study habits from the *first* of the nine weeks.

What Is the Parent's Role in Homework and Study?

I have a friend who, as a child, was moved frequently from one place to another because his father was in the Air Force. As a result, by second grade, he had been placed in a remedial reading group, which was quite embarrassing to him. His mother began to tutor him at home. Usually she would not allow him to go outside and play until his homework was all done. As a result of her dedicated efforts, he learned good study habits. When he got older, he had chores to do on Saturday. He also became actively involved in sports and church activities.

This young man went to the top of his class and stayed there, right through college (where he was an honor pre-med student) and on through medical school. Today he is a successful surgeon. He credits his academic success to his mother's hard-nosed attitude and unbending rule: "Work first — play later."

Here are ways you can support your child to help him develop good study habits and enjoy academic success:

- Instill in him an attitude that considers school work an important priority. It is part of our responsibility as parents to teach our children that hard work pays off. It is also our duty to be positive in our own attitude and to inspire self-confidence in our children. Every child should experience some success, however small, every day. Pay attention to what your child does *right*, and give genuine praise when it is due. "I appreciate your hard work; I'm proud of you," can mean a lot to a child. Don't bribe him to make better grades, and don't threaten him when he makes bad grades. (Low grades are, in fact, often an indicator of a learning gap or a need for special tutoring. Sometimes they reflect turmoil within the student or the family or both.)

- Be interested in *content*, in *what* your child is learning, not just in his grades. Rewards can be given, as a surprise and for effort. You can take your son or daughter out for pizza after an improved test score just as you would after a soccer game. It is great motivation to a child to hear his parent say, "I'm so proud of your hard work; let's go out and celebrate."

- Help your child learn to break large tasks into smaller steps. For example, if he has a long report to write, have him do the library work this week, and then write the paper next week. Suggest that he read a chapter a day to finish that lengthy novel on time. Planning ahead for a long-term project is crucial. Last-ditch efforts made late at night to get the assignment in just before the deadline draws the parent into too much involvement (so the dear one won't get a zero!), and the student learns nothing (except that Mom can always be depended on to bail him out!). It is better to let the student turn in an assignment late than to do it for him. Even if he has to suffer a bit, it may be worth it; next time he'll learn to plan ahead.

- Encourage your child to set realistic goals, like bringing his history grade up from a C to a B. You can help him discover how he learns best by having him make use of all three learning channels in his study. (See chapter on learning styles.)

- Encourage self-reliance and responsibility. Your child needs your support, but he also needs to do the homework himself! Remember, it's the student's work, not yours. Let him know that. It may take a little extra time, but if he has done a math problem incorrectly, point it out to him. Show him how to work it correctly if he truly can't figure it out for himself. Then let him correct the problem. If he has four glaring run-on sentences in his essay, call them to his attention, giving him an example of how to revise the paper — but let him make the revision. Encourage self-reliance — an "I can do it" attitude in your child.

- Teach your child concentration. Paying attention in class is a key to learning. Teach your child listening skills. Encourage him to sit close to the front of the classroom, if possible, and pay attention. Let him know that talking or passing notes in class while the teacher is instructing is not to be tolerated.

- Give your child responsibility at home. Teachers say that they can spot a student who has responsibility at home because he does better in class. Encourage your child to take responsibility for his belongings. Have him carry out a few daily chores at home. Require that he keep his room clean and well-organized. If you can instill a sense of personal responsibility in him now, you will have gone a long way toward helping your child become a success in school — and in life.

Parent: Homework Consultant

I like the title *consultant* to describe the parent's role. A consultant advises, helps plan strategy and makes suggestions for organizational changes.

A friend of ours in Texas hired a consultant to evaluate the method of operation of his clothing store and to make recommendations for improvements in every aspect of his business. By following the consultant's advice, our friend saved a great deal of money, made some important changes in his basic operation and got the business on a firm footing before the outbreak of an expected recession. As a result, he was able to survive — and even increase his share of the market — during a time when many less stable clothing businesses in the area were going bankrupt.

In the same way, you can provide your child the *tools* he will need to survive the changes and storms which may lie ahead of him in the future.

Tools for School Survival

Why do I use the word *survival*? At fifth grade, if your child enters middle school, as most do, he will go to as many as five to seven teachers a day (instead of being confined in a self-contained classroom, as he was in elementary school). He will have many things to remember, numerous assignments in many subjects to do and turn in the next day or on Friday or in two weeks. He will have to keep up with textbooks and workbooks, loose papers, and a flood of handouts from a variety of teachers.

With all of that responsibility — besides the noise and confusion of classes with 25 or more students in them, not to mention all the distractions and activities of everyday school life — just to survive takes no small amount of skill on the part of youngsters straight out of elementary school. Add to all of that frustration the stress of your child's own relationships, his inner feelings, his weaknesses and limitations. How is he ever going to stand the strain and keep it all straight? How can he possibly be prepared for every subject every day?

Here's how: as his consultant, you're going to teach your child some study strategies that will work for him. You're going to give him some resources for effective study. You're going to help him get organized. With this help from you, he will be launched on his way to school survival — and even more, to success.

To some children effective study techniques come naturally. Without being told, they seem to know to cover one side of the page, say the vocabulary words and their meanings out loud, and then check themselves by glancing at the correct answers. They naturally make lists and take good notes. But for most children, studying means nothing more than reading over the material once — and that just won't get the job done. Most children need to *do something* with the material if they are to ingest it, digest it, and then record it in a long-term memory framework from which it can be recalled at will. To do this, middle school students need to be helped to develop study strategies that work for them personally.

Then after your child has made it through middle school, he or she will arrive at that time around puberty when the adolescent body begins to change, the mind becomes a little scattered, and everything he or she has learned up to that point seems to be totally forgotten.

Junior high school requires many adjustments. Teachers report that there is more school failure at the junior high level than at any other stage in school life. There are physical changes, social changes, and peer pressures to contend with. In addition, the young person is expected to shift from concrete learning (the accumulation of facts) to analytical learning and critical thinking. More responsibility is required of him in his assignments. In the midst of these stressful transitions, many junior high school students find themselves lacking the organizational and study skills they need to survive. They may have done well in elementary school (especially if they were spoon-fed), but now that they are expected to take responsibility for their own learning, things begin to fall apart and their grades start to drop.

That's why it is so important that good study habits be firmly established in students before all these changes begin to take place. These habits are crucial if students are to stay on track and enjoy some measure of success and enjoyment of learning during the challenging junior high school years.

Our students can be motivated; they can understand and remember; they can learn to work without stress (all ingredients for success in school) — if we provide them *resources for study*. Following are some of these vital resources:

Proper Nutrition:

One of the basic resources of learning is good nutrition. Since it is extremely important that school children start the day right, one of the most effective things you can do to promote your child's school success is to serve him a good breakfast.

Children are not as alert and able to concentrate when they skip breakfast. A sugary breakfast like donuts and sugar-coated cereal adversely affects children's behavior and ability to focus. For many, it causes hyperactivity and restlessness. But the big "let-down" comes around 9:00 to 10:00 a.m. when much is demanded of students who may be feeling drowsy because of a sudden drop in their blood sugar.

Nutritionists agree that breakfast should contain an adequate amount of protein. But Jerry Gautreaux, a registered dietician, counsels parents, "Most of all, don't stereotype breakfast." Beside the usual eggs and toast fare, she suggests some healthy, whole, fresh-food alternatives to combine for a nutritious breakfast:

- soup or left-over pizza

- grilled cheese sandwich

- yogurt on granola with fruit

- English muffin covered with melted cheese

- brown rice with honey, raisins and cinnamon

- peanut butter on rice cakes

- fresh or frozen fruit salad with sunflower seeds

- pocket bread with almond butter and dates

- oatmeal with raisins or dried fruit

- toast with cream cheese and apricot jam

- macaroni and cheese

- ramen

At lunch time, encourage your child to pick the most nutritious food on the menu if he goes through the cafeteria line: he can select milk instead of punch or soda pop, salad instead of French fries. If you pack a brown-bag lunch for him, Ms. Gautreaux advises against getting stuck in a rut of potato chips and a bologna sandwich. Don't send candy bars or soft drinks: send one cookie, not four.

Many of the breakfast ideas above also work for lunch. You can make sandwiches on whole wheat bread, pocket bread or tortillas, filled with tuna salad, peanut butter, or cheese slices and avocado. Send some fresh fruit. Soup in a thermos with cheese and crackers; celery, carrot and apple sticks — all are good choices for a hearty lunch.

We can learn a lot from the typical Japanese mother who considers it a high priority to cook a fine breakfast for her family as part of her responsibility as "education mama." She also gets up early to fix an exquisite *o'bento* (a box lunch usually containing fried chicken, boiled eggs, rice, lotus roots, mint leaves, tomatoes, carrots, and fruit salad) to send with her child.

Practical School Supplies:

Your child needs an organized notebook — one with dividers and paper for each subject, a clip, and three-holed pockets. (Usually called "Pocket Divider Binder Refills," these pockets are great for organizing papers, notes and handouts for each subject. They can be purchased at any office supply store.) School children have a lot of paper to keep up with, and they need all the help they can get in this area.

Instead of requiring notebooks, one Texas middle school has found success with having each child provide a different-colored folder for each class. The folders must have pockets on the inside front and back, and three brads for paper. The children keep hand-outs in the front pocket and tests in the back. They take the right folder (with the subject written on the front cover with a large magic marker) to each class. As an alternative to a large notebook, a set of folders could work for some students. Often the teacher will advise students as to what type of classroom materials they will need.

A plastic zipper pocket for the front of the notebook — to hold pencils, erasable pens, paper-hole reinforcements, map pencils, a small pencil sharpener, and other supplies — is a necessity.

An assignment notebook is vital for writing down assignments in each class as the teacher gives them. Don't allow your child to rely on his memory (or imagination!) to keep track of his assignments until he gets home from school several hours later. Long-term assignments can be transferred to a big desk calendar at home.

For the student who has trouble getting assignments written into his assignment notebook:

1. Make up a weekly calendar sheet of his classes, with blocks for each subject and day of the week. Each week provide the student with a photocopy of this calendar to staple to the front of his notebook. When it's right there, he won't forget as easily to fill it in. (I have to give my daughter credit for this "assignment sheet

143

stapled on top of the notebook" idea. It has worked beautifully for her. What's important is to find a method that *works* for your child.)

2. Use yellow sticky notes to remind him to bring home the right books. How many times have you heard this? "I forgot my French and science books and I have homework to do in both of them!" The school is locked, of course. The solution to this problem is to have the student stick a yellow note inside each book he is going to need for homework that evening. At the end of the day, when he sees the yellow tab sticking out of the book, he will be reminded to bring it home.

3. If your child is failing to do his homework because he neglects to write down his assignments (and if he fails to respond to these other methods), there is one final alternative: an "account-ability sheet." On one sheet per day, the student writes down the assignment and takes it up for the teacher to initial at the end of each class. The homework sheet goes home at the end of the day; the parent checks it, and a small reward or token is given for completing the assignment successfully. I have seen this method work when others have failed. It helps the student become more responsible. Getting assignments done, he brings his grades up, feels better about himself and his ability, and builds a cycle of success instead of failure. Once he gets into the habit of keeping track of his assignments, he can transfer to a regular assignment book.

For young people who need a little extra guidance and motivation to get their school work done or to behave appropriately in class, a Periodic Progress Report (PPR) is a valuable resource. (For information, consult your school counselor, or write: Communications & Public Service, Boys Town, Nebraska, 68010.)

A *school supply shelf* is a time-saver at home. Either a cabinet shelf or a plastic bin can contain: extra ballpoint pens, pencils, erasers, paper, folders, and markers. Index cards, a stapler and staples, glue and paper clips are handy items to have available. Also, keep on hand two or three pieces of white posterboard for special projects. (This may save you a trip to the store at 10:00 p.m.) I get extra supplies at the first of the year and replenish the stock as necessary. That way, supplies are always on the shelf when needed. This is much better than having children borrowing supplies from one another or other students or not having what they need (some teachers take off points for not having the necessary school supplies).

A Place to Study:

Every person in the family should have a study or work space in the home. An organized desk in a relatively quiet place (television and radio off for most children), with good lighting, containers for supplies, and space to read and write is very helpful. Some children, however, study best at the kitchen table with a parent nearby (perhaps paying bills, reading, or writing a letter). Find the best place for your child's study.

Time to Study:

The writer of the biblical book of Ecclesiastes tells us that there is a time for every activity of life. (Eccl. 3:1.) Be sure you set a regular time for study in your home. Find out at what time of day your child does his best work, when his energy level is at its peak, and adjust his study time accordingly.

Most children need a break after school and before starting their homework. Their eyes need a rest from so much close work. Intellectually and emotionally they may be saturated with instructions, activities and the presence of people, so they may need a little unstructured time to "unwind."

The *kinesthetic learner* needs a break the most; at least thirty minutes outside running, playing, throwing a football — doing something active — before settling down to start his homework.

The *auditory learner* also needs a change of pace, like a walk or bike ride, but also a time to talk, because that's how he works out the frustrations, questions and events of his day — by verbalizing them. Right after school, maybe with a cup of hot chocolate, is a good time to visit. He may also enjoy listening to records or just playing.

The *visual learner* may immediately retreat to a book, newspaper, or the television set to "unwind," but can also benefit from getting outside to shoot baskets, jump rope or take a walk.

These are important moments, right after school. Often the child will have something on his mind from his school day. It may be troubling or exciting, but it will come bubbling out *if there is someone there to listen* and to ask him, "How was your day?" Some of the best chats my children and I have ever had together have been right after school.

In a recently released survey of 2,000 parents and 1,000 teachers, Louis Harris and Associates, Inc. reported that 25 percent of the parents interviewed said that they leave their children alone every day between the end of school and 5:30 or 6:00 p.m. (And 41 percent said they leave their children home alone at least once a week during this time.)

For these children, an after-school program (which includes time for play and doing homework, with extra help available if needed) provided through the YMCA, church, or school can be very helpful. A neighbor or grandparent who can be there for the child after school could be an alternative. If your child must stay home alone, leave suggestions on the chalkboard for how he can spend his time. Also make sure he has access to at least one parent by telephone. Ask your child's teacher if a Homework Hot-Line is available in your city. If so, leave the number by the phone. (See Chapter 10 for more information on the Homework Hot-Line.)

After a snack and break, the young child can sit down, set the kitchen timer for 20 or 30 minutes (depending on his age and attention span) and begin his homework. He can take the hardest subject and tackle it first: "Let's see if I can get these ten problems done before the timer goes off." Then after that work is done he can take perhaps a five-minute break for water, to stretch or go to the bathroom, and then it's back to the next subject for 20 or 30 minutes. For most elementary children, this will be enough time to finish all their work. If necessary, the last study period could be delayed until after dinner.

If you have a child in elementary school, you may want to ask his teacher how much time his homework should normally take. If he is getting sidetracked or is extremely slow in finishing his work, ask the teacher for suggestions. If there is a need to study for a test, you can pose the questions to your child orally, make flash cards, or use some of the memorizing strategies to help him study.

The evening meal, with the whole family sitting down around the table, praying together, and enjoying each other's presence, is a special time. No conflict, tattling, or anger should be allowed to spoil this family time. You can each share news of the day, getting practice in listening and talking in turn. Having dinner together is a very stabilizing factor in family life.

After dinner is a good time for reading aloud. Or homework can be begun (if it hasn't already been started) around the kitchen table or desk. Later, if television has been curbed on school nights, perhaps there will be time for a game, or for putting some pieces in a big jigsaw puzzle that has been left out for the family to work on. Children can hopefully have time to "parachute down" and relax before bedtime. A time of closeness, togetherness and communication with Mom or Dad before going to sleep can be highly valuable to a growing child. And, of course, the child needs adequate sleep for his age, physical condition and individual needs.

In the morning, it is important for the child to wake (at a regular time) to a nourishing breakfast, and a big dose of expressed love and encouragement: "I love you! God bless you! Have a good day!" Most children have a six- to eight-hour day ahead, and they need rest, support, preparation, and physical and emotional nourishment in order to meet all the demands that will be placed upon them during that time away from home.

Time spent developing strong study skills while your child is in grades one through six is an investment which will save you much time and frustration later on. The child who learns responsibility, organization and good study habits will, by his junior high school years, be quite independent, confident and able to handle the challenges ahead.

In the next chapter, we will discuss helps for memorization and studying for tests.

Chapter 12

STRATEGIES FOR STUDY

Teaching your child a few key *study strategies* can help him master the building blocks of information and concepts he is presented at school and on which he will be tested. Many of these strategies are most useful for junior high and high school students, but, with certain adaptations, they can also be applied to middle school students.

Just like a coach, standing on the sidelines, laying strategies, offering encouragement, correcting mistakes and providing direction when needed, you are going to "coach" your child to success in study.

Taking Notes

Taking good notes helps the student retain what he is supposed to remember from class lectures and presentations. It also helps him stay alert, interested and "tuned in," because he is actively doing something with the information being presented, rather than just passively sitting through a lecture or discussion. (When required to sit and listen for a long period of time, visual and kinesthetic learners, especially, tend to become bored and restless; unless actively stimulated, they will "tune out" mentally and begin to daydream, doodle, or cause problems in class.)

Teach your child to:

- Listen for teacher cues. If the teacher writes facts or concepts on the board, they are probably important and should be written down. She might give verbal clues like: "*Three primary causes* of the Civil War are...," or, "*The purpose* of the Bill of Rights is...." If confused about the most important points, your child should ask the teacher about them.

- Take notes — either in a basic outline form or on index cards. (If you have a method for taking notes that works for you, share it with your child!)

- Review his notes at a later time. He should learn to jot words in the left margin. It is also helpful to use a yellow highlighter to mark important points in the notes to review while studying. When it comes time for a test on the material, the student should study his notes by reading over them several days in advance, then rewriting, discussing or tape recording them.

Reading and Summarizing a Chapter

Reading over new course material the night before the teacher's presentation and explanation of it in class greatly increases the student's understanding and interest. He is then more familiar with the subject under discussion, and thus more receptive to it.

Teach your child that, when reading a chapter for any subject, he should *ask questions* about the material: who, what, when, where, and how. He should learn to read a section at a time, noting key headings and topic sentences. He should look for main points, asking:

- "What is the main idea in this paragraph?"

- "What am I supposed to be learning?"

- "What do I need to remember?"

It is helpful for the student to highlight the answers to these questions in the textbook or to write them down in his own words in an outline or list.

He should pay particular attention to headings, introductions, new vocabulary words, and summaries at the end of chapters. Charts, review questions, and glossaries are good aids to understanding the material. A good study technique for the visual child, when reading a chapter, is to make a drawing of the main idea and supporting information:

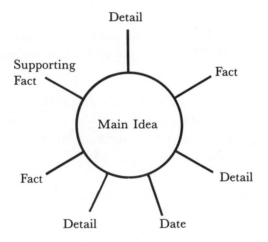

Memorizing Magic

Your child can learn to take the drudgery out of memorization by making a game of it. There is a place for problem-solving and divergent thinking, but students need recall of facts as a foundation for these more advanced mental operations.

151

> "Memorizing simplifies the process of recalling information and allows its use to become automatic. Understanding and critical thought can then build on this base of knowledge and fact. Indeed, the more sophisticated mental operations of analysis, synthesis, and evaluation are impossible without rapid and accurate recall of bodies of special knowledge."
>
> *What Works*[1]

Some things, like multiplication tables, correct spelling of words, dates in history, vocabulary in foreign languages, and parts of speech must be memorized.

Effective memorization strategies link the known to the unknown, make use of mental pictures and humor, and even set information to music.

Mnemonics, or memory devices, can make memorizing faster and more enjoyable. (Do you remember repeating "Every Good Boy Does Fine" to recall the order of the notes on the treble staff: EGBDF?) To remember the names of the Great Lakes, just think of the word *HOMES:* Huron, Ontario, Michigan, Erie and Superior. If your child has to memorize the eight parts of speech, he can make an acrostic like this:

Nancy   (Noun)

Picks   (Pronoun)

Very   (Verb)

Ample   (Adverb)

Apples   (Adjective)

If   (Interjection)

Canning   (Conjunction)

Properly   (Preposition)

Whether it involves learning key formulas, cities and state capitals, or other basic facts, you and your child can make up your own devices to increase retention and jog the memory.

The following is a practical guide you can share with your child to help him learn the correct spelling of a word:

1. Look at the word and say it.

2. Close your eyes and think what the word looks like.

3. Say it, and try to spell it.

4. Open your eyes, look at the word, and check your spelling.

5. Cover the word and write it several times.

6. Close your eyes again and spell the word aloud.

Studying for Tests

Besides the learning style methods for studying test material (see Chapter 3), here are some guidelines for successful test-taking:

- Have the student plan ahead and avoid cramming. Three nights before the test, have him review his class notes. The second night he should tape record the main points, or practice the basic information by using flashcards or rereading the notes. The night before the test, have him make out a practice test and take it; you should ask him the questions orally, if possible.

- Have the student note the type of test the teacher usually gives. Most teachers have a pattern to the multiple-choice, true-false, fill-in-the-blank or essay questions they ask. Often the teacher will announce before the test the type of questions which will be on it.

- Encourage the student to think about the most important concepts and information the teacher will be looking for when he makes out the test. Have him learn all the vocabulary words. Give him a trial test; then grade it, circling the points he needs to work on. If the test involves making up answers, such as sentences with the eight parts of speech, have the student do his own work rather than relying on you or the textbook to supply them for him.

- Encourage the student to study with a friend: My son's biology teacher is a strong advocate of study groups. He finds that students learn so much from each other. (I agree: Some of the most productive study times I ever had were those spent with two chemistry classmates.) Each person in the study group can write down the *top ten questions* he or she thinks will most likely be on the exam. Once the most important questions have been listed, then each member of the group can look up the answers and note them, either orally or on paper. The group can then pool their information, discuss each question, and determine the best answer to it.

- Ask the student to teach the material to you. This provides a good means of reinforcement of the information, and a boost to his confidence.

After the test is over, when the score is brought home, if it is low, don't say "I told you so." Avoid criticizing the student or laying blame for his poor showing. Sometimes the amount of time and effort put into study is not reflected in the final grade, especially in the first stages of the development of study strategies. Studying is a good way for the young person to learn to be persistent instead of letting down or giving up.

If the grade is lower than the child had expected, encourage him to press on. Help him prepare for the next test. Urge him to keep up with his daily lessons. If he is still discouraged, perhaps try a different set of strategies, consult with his teacher or get tutoring help if it is needed.

Help: Where Do I Get it?

Your son or daughter needs to learn how to get help for difficult learning tasks. Sometimes it may be hard to ask for it, but the best and brightest students know where to turn for assistance when they need it — and they don't hesitate to ask.

Even in elementary school, children need to know that the teacher is there to help them, but that they must *ask* for that help. Sometimes that takes a bit of encouragement and a brave heart. To avoid embarrassment, students may want to go by after class, or before or after school, to talk to the teacher or to ask a question. Usually the teacher is glad to help and may even come to feel more positive toward the student (rather than assuming that his poor showing is evidence of a lack of interest or effort).

Let your student know he can also get help from:

- an older brother or sister who has taken the course.

- Mom or Dad. Often parents have complementary areas of skill. In our family, when our children need help, I tutor them in English, history, or language, and my husband helps them with their math and science.

- a friend of the family who is a retired teacher or a specialist in a certain field of knowledge.

- a tutor, either from the university or one recommended by a teacher or another parent.

- a community learning center which provides evaluation and/or tutoring services.

Writing and Editing
Successful Papers

Help your student develop a step by step approach to writing, realizing that writing is a *process*. This process consists of the following outlined steps. Share each of these with your son or daughter. Then note the Parent Response which provides suggestions for facilitating that stage of the writing process.

Prewriting:

Perhaps the most important step of all, prewriting gives the student something to do besides staring at a blank piece of paper. Batting ideas around, thinking about the topic and talking about possible subjects on which to write are all part of the prewriting process. For an auditory learner, ideas start to flow once he can talk about the topic. Freewriting is also a good prewriting method. In freewriting, the student writes without hesitation the first things that come to mind when he considers the topic. Some people like to draw diagrams of their thoughts, clustering ideas into a pattern as they emerge. Out of all these efforts, there will begin to arise a subject to write about.

PARENT RESPONSE: You can help your child at this point by actively participating with him as he "brainstorms" for topics to write on and ideas he wants to develop. You can listen to him and talk with him about his ideas. Encourage freewriting. (It would be nice if prewriting activities were entirely done in class, but unfortunately, many times the topic the student is to write about is assigned to him by the teacher.)

Writing the First Draft:

After reading over his notes and freewriting, the student should begin to organize his ideas into a workable form for presentation. This form should include a definite beginning (introduction of the topic to be discussed), middle (discussion), and ending (conclusions drawn from the discussion).

If outside research is needed, now is the time for the student to go to the library to find the necessary reference materials. From these he draws any resource information needed, recording it on notecards, being careful to note on each card the source of the information being used. These sources will be listed at the end of the paper in a bibliography.

A scratch outline usually helps order thoughts. After organizing the material to be presented, the student begins to write the rough draft, concentrating first on getting the main ideas down on paper rather than worrying about perfect mechanics.

PARENT RESPONSE: Let the student know that this is not a final draft he is writing. Encourage him to get the main thoughts down on paper in this first draft.

Revising:

Before revising the first draft, it is best to let it "sit and get cold." If the student doesn't have a day or so to let the paper "sit," he should at least go do some other homework or take a short break before continuing to work on it.

When he comes back, he should read the first draft as if he were a reader who knew nothing at all about the subject under discussion. At this stage, he should concentrate on *content*, considering the purpose of the assignment. For example, if it is a personal experience essay he is writing, he should ask himself if the reader will be able to relate to the incident from the details presented and the scenes described.

It is best that he read the paper aloud for meaning and organization. It is also helpful, at this point, to have someone else read it. The student could *tape record the paper and listen as it is played back, marking it as he listens*. He now begins to improve his writing, making sure that it says what he wants it to say. Any obscure sentences or difficult passages are deleted or rewritten. This revision produces the second draft of the paper.

In my first year of teaching freshman English, I had a huge number of essays to read and mark. To encourage my students to write, I tried to make at least one positive comment on each paper (in addition to the other necessary notes and comments). To do that, I found that I had to think ahead and prepare myself mentally and emotionally; otherwise I would be so overwhelmed by all the errors I saw, I would become negative. To help me remain positive in my approach, I compiled a list of possible compliments, which really helped spark genuine encouragement. Here are examples of positive comments you can make about your child's writing efforts:

- "Your main idea is great; tell me more about it."

- "Good word choice: your message is clear and to the point."

- "Your writing makes me feel happy (excites me, intrigues me, moves me deeply, evokes pleasant memories, paints a beautiful picture...)."

- "Your strongest point is..."

- "I like your choice of topics."

- "The way you combined these two ideas was imaginative (clever, ingenious, novel...)."

- "Your organization (dialogue, characterization, imagery...) is excellent."

Once you have complimented the student on some area of his writing which he seems to do well, then you can begin to ask gentle, helpful questions to point out areas that need further work. (Remember how sensitive young people can be; avoid making any statements that may discourage the young writer or crush his fragile self-confidence.) Help the student learn to evaluate his own paper and to decide on constructive changes which can be made to it. Be selective in your choice of areas to deal with: don't try to correct everything at once. Writing teachers call this process "conferring." Here are the types of questions you may want to ask:

- "What is your favorite sentence, (paragraph, part) of the essay?"

- "What part was most difficult to write?"

- "I was not sure what you meant in this part; could you clarify it?"

- "Is this paragraph on one topic?"

- "Could you write a concluding sentence to really wrap up all your ideas?"

- "What details could you add here?"

Editing:

Have the student read his paper again, checking for punctuation, spelling, sentence structure, etc. *If he reads it aloud, errors will be apparent to him.* Reading with pencil in hand, he can mark these errors, making note of any structural changes needed. Then, the entire paper can be rewritten or typed, in a neat, readable form, with all the errors corrected and the changes made. This is the third and final draft. (Note: *It is always a good idea to carefully proofread this final copy.*)

PARENT RESPONSE: As you teach your child to edit, focus on just a few mechanical errors at a time. Do not correct the paper with a red pen. Do not come across as judgmental or critical. Stay positive. Here are some suggested questions you can use to help point out to your child any errors in grammar, punctuation and spelling in his writing:

- "Do you think a different word might work better here?"

- "Do you think this is one sentence or two sentences run together? Where might a punctuation mark go? Which mark?"

- "Are you sure this word is spelled correctly? Why don't we look it up in the dictionary?"

Avoid trying to *fix* the paper for your child. Let ownership of the paper remain with the child. The process of his learning how to write, revise and edit is the most important thing, and that process takes time to develop.

Sharing:

Sharing the finished paper with someone else (by reading it aloud at dinnertime, making it into a little book, including it in a school library journal, posting it on the bulletin board or submitting it to a young people's magazine) is very encouraging to the writer. Many times it inspires his next writing project.

The student who learns to write clearly and to edit and revise his own writing has a head start on success in every school subject. Answering essay test questions becomes easier, and writing class papers more enjoyable. (For more ideas on how to develop writing skills, see Chapter 7, "Help Your Child Become a Lifelong Writer.")

As you share these study methods and organizational strategies with your child, remember that your goal is to help him learn to solve problems and to accept responsibility for his own schoolwork. Most of all, you will be teaching him how to study and instilling in him a love for learning which, hopefully, will stay with him for the rest of his life.

Recommended Reading

Louise Colligan. *Scholastics's A + Junior Guide to Studying.* New York: Scholastic Books, 1987.

Louise Colligan. *Scholastic's A + Guide to Taking Tests.* New York: Scholastic Books, 1982.

Homework: Helping Students Achieve. American Association of School Administrators: Arlington, Virginia, 1985.

Parent's Guide to the Periodic Progress Report and What to Do If Your Child Is an Underachiever in School. Communications and Public Service: Boys Town, Nebraska 68010.

Footnotes

[1]*What Works: Research About Teaching and Learning,* United States Department of Education: William J. Bennett, Secretary, 1986, p. 37.

Chapter 13

IT'S CONFERENCE TIME: HOW TO COMMUNICATE WITH TEACHERS

Open House

As I raced to my son's next class, the heel of my shoe turned and I slipped on the slick hall floor. A man walking by grabbed me just before I hit the floor.

"Are you all right?' he asked.

"No," I answered, "but I'll be okay."

We only had five minutes between bells to find the classes, and this was a big high school building. My foot hurt like crazy, and I knew I was going to be late.

Hurriedly, I slid into the seat closest to the door in my son's history class, just in time to hear the teacher say, "I like to teach ninth-graders, but I'm certainly glad they have to go home to you!" Teenagers, she explained, are "a handful." Oh, how I knew that — or at least was beginning to find it out! But this time, I was on the other side of the desk, sitting in one of the small wooden chairs my son sat in every day.

Open houses, usually held early in the school year or once in the fall and spring, are one way to meet your child's teacher(s) and to start becoming involved with his school. Recent research shows that there is a strong correlation between parent involvement in the schools and student achievement. Parents and teachers are partners in education, and if we are going to work for the best interests of our children, we need to know our partners.

At open house, parents may see a sampling of their children's work. At all levels, each teacher gives a presentation, explaining the curriculum and what the students are learning in her class. Often she will explain the grading scale, homework requirements, and her goals for the school year. Parents get a sense of the teacher's expectations. But most teachers don't have time to discuss individual students at open house; instead, it is a get-acquainted time.

I have heard teachers say to parents, "Don't believe everything you hear about me, and I won't believe everything I hear about you!" Effective communication between home and school is vital to avoid misunderstandings — or to clear them up when they do occur. Despite all of our best efforts to make our educational system effective, the truth is that schools are imperfect institutions run by imperfect people who must work with imperfect students. Mistakes will be made by all parties involved. But together we can identify problems and work to solve them before they become detrimental to our children's progress.

You may be thinking, "But my child is doing above average work." Even if your child is doing well in school, it helps for you to get to know his teacher and keep the lines of communication open for future needs which may arise. You want to know that your child is being challenged and not just sliding by. You can gain important insights into your child's development and how he interacts with peers. You will discover skills that need to be reinforced at home, or enrichment that you can provide outside of the school environment. The teacher needs your interest and support because education is a team effort, and you, the parent, are a vital part of the team.

The Parent-Teacher Conference

Another means of establishing communication between home and school is the parent-teacher conference. Schools generally set aside a certain day for these conferences, but if there is a legitimate need you can request a meeting with your child's teacher at any time during the year. Here are some guidelines to help make it a productive time of working together:

1. If possible, both parents should attend the conference. With both parents present, you can get a more balanced picture of the child and his school situation.

2. Be aware that nervousness or anxiety may surface because you are meeting with someone you don't know who teaches your child every day and is "in charge." Realize that these feelings are normal.

"Butterflies raced in my stomach before the conference with Jennifer's teachers," said Carolyn. "I was so nervous I couldn't think of what I wanted to say. I was afraid that the teacher was going to tell me Jennifer had a reading problem or talked too much or something. I didn't know *what* she was going to say, and I didn't know if I really wanted to hear it."

For some people, the educational setting and jargon is intimidating. If your own school days held any painful experiences for you, old memories may rise and cause you to become defensive.

165

Be patient with yourself and know that some anxiety is normal. The better you get to know the teacher, the less awkward the conferences will be.

3. Be on time and prepared by having talked with your child in advance, asking how things are going at school, what he likes best, and if he has any problems.

4. Say something positive to affirm the teacher's efforts. Most teachers work very hard and need encouragement too! Express thanks for the teacher's efforts in working with your child, for some interesting project the class has done, or for some class activity your child particularly enjoyed.

5. Bring a list of questions you may have or subjects you would like to discuss. Here are some good questions to ask at a conference:

- "How is my child doing in class?"

- "Is he consistent about turning in classwork or homework?"

- "Does he use time well? What are his work habits like?"

- "Does he pay attention? How is his behavior in class?"

- "How well does he get along with other children?"

- "Does he have friends? Does he seem to be happy?"

- "What can be done at home to reinforce or support what you are doing here at school?"

- "Are there any learning activities you can suggest to be done at home?"

6. Remember, a conference is a time for both parent and teacher to talk *and* listen. Be tactful but honest. Let the teacher know about any health problems or handicaps, any recent crisis or change at home that may affect your child's learning. In addition, you can share your goals for your child. You can gain valuable insight into the child's development by listening carefully

as the teacher describes how he functions in class and how he is progressing both academically and socially.

7. *If there is a problem* that you know about, don't wait until it becomes severe before you call the teacher to schedule a conference. Don't wait until your child is failing! If you are concerned about something, write a note or call to request a parent-teacher conference.

Then, when you and the teacher meet together, try to determine just what the cause of the problem is. Often it will stem from a single situation in one class that is negatively affecting the child's whole school experience. It may be that he is disorganized or just behind in math. You as the parent may see one side of the puzzle, and the teacher the other. Begin by sharing with the teacher what is happening at home, describing what feedback you are getting from the student. Then ask, "What is happening with my child here at school? What do you see" By putting your views together with those of the teacher, you will likely get a more complete picture of the situation.

Working together, parent and teacher can identify the problem and discover ways to help the child. Be careful not to blame the teacher. Avoid an adversary relationship. As one teacher said, "Some parents see a parent-teacher conference as a meeting of opposing forces." Don't approach your child's teacher in a negative frame of mind. Instead, let your attitude be, "What can we do together to further the best interests of this child?"

8. Follow up on the conference. The teacher may suggest some home learning activities she believes will strengthen the child's skills. Try your best to follow through on these suggestions and then get back with the teacher to share the results. Show interest in school work, not just at report card and conference time, but throughout the school year. Encourage your child to respect the teacher and cooperate with her, to be quiet and attentive in class, to communicate with the teacher when a problem arises or when he need helps, and certainly to communicate with you.

There are many other ways to be a partner in your child's education. Find some school-related activity you would enjoy participating in or helping with. Some parents like to organize school carnivals, while others like to help in the computer room or library.

Even working mothers and fathers can find time to become involved. The Durham County School System in North Carolina reports one of the highest percentages of working mothers in the United States. Yet the school system recruits 200 volunteers a year under a PTA Partnership Program. The Yarmouth, Maine, elementary schools have over 150 parent volunteers who work with children in the computer lab, type their stories and transform them into books in the publishing center, work in the library, teach crafts at the annual Colonial Crafts Day, and serve in many other areas of school life.

Other school systems are discovering ingenious ways for parents to become partners with the school. Here are some ways you can get involved in your child's education:

- Volunteer to help with field trips, make materials for the classroom or assist in class.

- Volunteer to help with class parties.

- Volunteer to provide one-on-one tutoring to students with learning disabilities.

- Go to school one day and have lunch with your child in the cafeteria. (Check with the school office first; most schools welcome a parent guest for lunch, if previously scheduled.)

- Join and participate in the local parent-teacher association, which affords other opportunities for involvement: raising funds for needed equipment, helping in the library, supervising in the cafeteria, and taking part in many other supportive activities.

- Attend school sports events, awards assemblies, and fine arts presentations such as musical programs, stage productions and art shows.

Classroom Observation

One of the best means of parent-teacher contact is visiting the classroom to observe how your child is being taught. You never know what is going on in the classroom, the teacher's style and method of teaching, until you sit quietly in the back of her room and watch the proceedings. "This first-hand observation shows parents how the teacher teaches and gives parents ideas on what they can do at home," say researchers in *What Works.*[1]

One year my husband and I became concerned about reports we were constantly receiving of poor discipline, general chaos, and teacher tardiness in our son's junior high school class. So my husband called the principal and in a very diplomatic tone of voice asked if he could spend an afternoon at school. He was graciously allowed to do so. First he had lunch with our son, then he went through the rest of the school day with him. Although he had to take off from work, the insights and results my husband gained in his visit were so valuable he considered it time well spent.

Often the only time we visit our children's classrooms is to drop off cookies for the Valentine's Day party. I have heard parents say, "Johnny would just die of embarrassment if I came up to his school." Actually Johnny may not mind at all. Even if he does mind, it would be better for him to be a little embarrassed now than for his parents to discover at the end of the school year that there had been a big problem which could have been solved with a little personal attention.

Here are some guidelines for effective classroom observation:

1. Notify the principal ahead of time that you would like to observe the class in order to get a clearer picture of what is expected of your child and to better help him at home. I have never known of a parent's being denied permission to observe his child in class.

2. Before arriving in the classroom, check to make sure the principal has notified the teacher of your visit.

3. Arrive on time, at the beginning of class rather than right in the middle, so you don't disrupt instruction.

4. If you would like, ask for a copy of the main textbooks so you can follow along with the class.

5. Sit in the back of the room and be very quiet.

6. From the schedule on the board (if there is one), note how the teacher and students spend their time. Also try to determine the teacher's learning style because a teacher usually teaches out of her own learning style. Here are some clues:

A *visual teacher* puts up lots of colorful bulletin boards and displays (even in upper grades) and uses a variety of visual teaching materials such as written instructions and handouts. She may even use an overhead projector. Usually she does not provide a great deal of oral explanation and may quickly grow weary of answering oral questions. (All this is great if your child is a visual learner.)

An *auditory teacher* usually keeps a little plainer classroom, one that is functional but attractive. She provides lots of verbal explanation and welcomes discussion. There is more talking about the lesson, reasons for activities, and questions. The students may be allowed to study together or participate in small-group discussions. The auditory teacher usually gives instructions for class assignments or homework *orally*, rather than in written form. (That's fine as long as your child is also auditory; otherwise he may not get all the directions and may fail to follow through on his work.)

A *kinesthetic teacher* will usually place an emphasis on hands-on learning activities — more doing and personal involvement on everyone's part. Rather than having all the chairs arranged in the traditional back-to-front order, all facing the teacher's desk, she may prefer an open classroom, with several circular "learning centers" scattered about the room. She allows for more physical movement than other teachers, relies on demonstrations rather than explanations, and assigns projects and posters for reinforcement of her students' learning. It is a real treat for a kinesthetic child to have a kinesthetic teacher! (It may not, however, be the ideal learning environment for the visual or auditory learner.)

Being aware of the learning-teaching style of your child's teacher is valuable. Although teachers are being encouraged to allow for varied learning styles in their classrooms, sometimes your child will have a teacher whose teaching style is just the opposite of his own way of receiving and understanding information. If your child is a kinesthetic learner and his teacher uses primarily visual and auditory strategies, it can be a prime source of frustration for the child, perhaps resulting in a low level of achievement. By classroom observation, you can note any gaps in learning style and better determine what you can do to help fill those gaps at home. Perhaps you can even suggest some methods of study and classroom coping strategies which will help your child adapt. He needs to adjust to a variety of teaching styles, and you can give him the tools to do so. (See Chapter 3 for more information on learning styles.)

7. When you leave, don't forget to thank the teacher, saying something positive to her before you go.

One mother found that a good time to observe her child's classroom for a short period was when she came to the school to give a birthday party or attend a PTA committee meeting. She would go a little early and watch the teacher and students interact, observing how her child related to the other students in the class.

You will get a much better and more realistic grasp of your child's school experience by actually visiting his class while it is in session. So much of what we know of school is hearsay; sometimes we need a first-hand view.

Support, encourage and pray for the teachers, administrators and students of your child's school. Remember that many problems can be prevented by keeping in touch. With good communication between his parent and his teacher, aided by your active interest

and cooperation, school will be a much more positive experience
for your child.

Footnotes

[1]*What Works: Research About Teaching and Learning*, United States Department of Education,
William J. Bennett, Secretary, 1986, p. 19.

Chapter 14

SCHOOL'S OUT —
MIND'S OPEN: CURES FOR
THE SUMMERTIME BLUES

Living History

Row after row of square grey markers covered a green Mississippi hill; towering over the Confederate and Union graves were huge magnolia trees. From this vantage point in the Vicksburg National Military Park, we gazed out over the wide Mississippi River.

"Dad, look at the graves of all the soldiers who died in just the spring seige," Chris said, almost in a whisper. Suddenly the number of men who had fought at Vicksburg was not just an abstract fact in an American history book. Instead, as we read the names of the officers and men killed in that bloody engagement, there begin to sink into our minds the sobering reality of the terrible loss their families must have felt.

As we walked through trenches, crouched in replicas of shelters, and drove along the miles of battle lines across which Union and Confederate troops faced each other, and behind which they fought and died, we sensed the enormity of the struggle represented by just this one vast Civil War battlefield.

Our late May morning visit to the Vicksburg Military Park was an experience which involved all of the learning styles of our children, making history come alive for them as no mere two-dimensional book could ever do. And our two-hour interlude on the way to the seashore was a reminder of how enriching travel can be to a child's education, as he *sees, does* and thus *remembers!*

Receiving information through all three learning channels — auditory, visual and kinesthetic — all of us remembered and better understood basic information about the American Civil War:

- why it was fought
- who its opposing forces were
- how and why Vicksburg became a focal point of it
- what happened in its skirmishes and battles
- what its outcome was

At the Vicksburg National Military Park, the best documented Civil War battlefield in the United States, with over 1,500 markers, exhibits, and monuments, there was plenty of opportunity for the *visual* learner to soak up interesting history: We saw war-torn trenches and twenty huge iron cannons used by the Union forces to hurl shot and shell against the Confederate defenders of the city. We saw Confederate cannons and artillery pieces, and the restored Union ironclad, the *USS Cairo*. Sunk on December 12, 1862, raised and restored a hundred years later, the antique warship gave us insight into the U.S. Navy of the 1860s. In the park's visitor's center we saw an interpretative movie of the 47-day seige of Vicksburg, the last Confederate stronghold on the Mississippi

River. And when we stood on the two-hundred-foot bluff above the muddy Mississippi, we could understand why Lincoln had called Vicksburg the key to Union victory in the west.

There were also plenty of interaction facts for the *auditory* learner. For only $1.75 we bought a great guidebook entitled *Vicksburg — On Your Own: An Illustrated Guide to the Battlefield.* This helpful self-guide to the national military park included a siege map, pictures then and now, and a detailed description of the action which had taken place at various points along the miles-long seige lines which formed a semi-circle around the entire port city. Now and then we would read aloud from the guidebook as we made our way along the sweeping battlelines.

As we watched the movie, we heard thunderous cannons; as we drove along the battlefield drive, we took turns reading signs and markers and the inscriptions on the various battle monuments erected by the states represented in the gigantic struggle. We read about the opposing forces and their leaders and the position of their troops. We discussed the reasons for the Union thrust against Vicksburg, its importance to both sides, and the consequences of its ultimate fall. Bits and pieces of Civil War history our children had learned in school came together into a clearer picture as they began to grasp the sweep and scope of this whole epic struggle.

For the *kinesthetic* learner, there was plenty to touch and do. Poking our heads into every nook and cranny of the *USS Cairo* gave us a fascinating glimpse into the everyday life of the Civil War sailor. As we walked through the fields where Confederate fortifications had been erected, we could visualize the hand-to-hand confrontation which took place between the two armies. We could imagine the deafening roar as thousands of muskets and hundreds of cannons poured forth their deadly thunder. The children could sit on the artillery pieces and picture their crews working feverishly to load, fire and reload. They could touch both Union and Confederate monuments and feel the pride of each state in their "native sons" who had fought and died for the cause they believed in.

And as we drove east on evergreen-lined Interstate 20, headed toward Jackson and the Alabama border, the kids took turns writing postcards picked out at the Vicksburg park. Alison wrote to Mr. Andrews, her favorite counselor at school, describing what she had seen: "In Mississippi we went to a neat museum and tour all about the Civil War. And if you look on the front of the card you can see the actual cannons they used and the man in the monument is one of the leaders! Then at the souvenir place I got some Confederate $500 bills. Have a good summer! Love, Alison."

Justin wrote one of his friends: "We're traveling from Vicksburg to Jackson. While in Vicksburg, we saw monuments, battlefield areas and a film on the battles. We also saw a huge graveyard of Confederate and Union soldiers. FACT: One of the Union front lines during the battle stretched 8 miles! The weather is a lot more humid and hot than in OKLAHOMA, imagine that!"

As you can see, travel provides tremendous opportunities to learn history: to see, hear and do helps children to understand what would otherwise be distant and abstract. And travel doesn't have to be to some place far away. There are many places with interesting history, science and literary possibilities right in your own backyard! Many cities have hands-on science museums for young people, and each community has its own special landmarks. When you do visit a museum or historical site, discuss what you are seeing. Make your child responsible for sharing orally with others about the outing, writing letters or relating stories about the trip.

Before a planned vacation, write to the department of tourism of each state you will be visiting and request information on areas of interest, especially living history centers. Involve your child in map study and historical research of the locale in which you are planning to spend your family trip.

Your child can keep a travel journal, which not only records wonderful memories to look back on, but is great for developing writing fluency. (For more information on travel journals, see the chapter on writing skills.) Recently a friend of mine found the travel journal she had kept of a cross-country trip she took with her parents in the 1950s — a real treasure to share with her daughter.

Travel Box

There are many ways to keep your children entertained, happy and learning while traveling, whether it is on a short trip to Grandma's or a long trip through several states. I would like to share some of my favorites with you.

I have a plastic container which I call the "travel box." In it are pocket games like Yahtzee, Scrabble, Connect Four, and checkers. Auto bingo cards are fun to include, as well as two packs of cards for playing Gin Rummy, King's Corner, Twenty-One and other card games. A stack of Bible quiz cards, tape-recorded books of C.S. Lewis' *Chronicles of Narnia*, and sing-along tapes are also included.* Pencils, pens and paper are there for drawing and doodling, and for playing dots, tic-tac-toe, hangman and mystery pictures (one person makes the first stroke of a picture and the others have to guess what he is going to draw; each time they guess incorrectly he gets to add another stroke). Crossword puzzles, word-finders, math puzzles and new paperback books round out our "survival box." This kit stays packed and ready for the next trip.

These resources provide fun and help pass the long hours of riding. At the same time they enhance children's learning. Family car trips can be a great time for togetherness rather than claustrophobia; conflicts are minimized when boredom is banished!

Here are some more of our favorite "cures" for the "backseat blues":

Geography: The first player begins by naming a country, state, city or geographical area. (Or the game can be played with just states and cities.) The next player has to name a place which begins with the last letter of the one just given. If anyone repeats an answer,

---

* See appendix for a list of books on tape resources.

or cannot think of a new one, he is out. The last person still naming correctly wins the game.

Categories: To a clapped beat, each person names a brand of automobile, a species of animal, a type of fruit or vegetable, or an item from some other category. When a player fails to name a new item, or repeats one already named, he is out of the game. The last one left wins.

Name That Tune: One person hums a familiar tune and everyone else tries to guess what it is. Whoever guesses right gets to hum next!

It is also a good idea on a long trip to take along a book the whole family will enjoy. Read aloud one chapter a day, then have a rest time.

On our family trips, we also like to read riddles and try to guess the answers, make a list of the license plates from different states we see (on a long trip, we try to see if we can spot one from every state in the union), let the children study the road maps and figure how far we still have to go (it's always farther than we wish!), and play I Spy.

When traveling, remember to take along your sense of humor, and enjoy the time you spend together.

Vacation Time: Progression or Regression?

Between the time school ends for summer and when it resumes in the fall, most children have far too few learning experiences. Television watching usually increases during the "lazy, hazy days of summer." As their minds go "out to pasture," many young people get "rusty." They return to school in September having forgotten much of the factual information they learned the year before. Even worse, they lose some of their important learning skills.

But research has shown that children who have some at-home learning activities during the summer months do not suffer either regression or boredom. I have found that children don't want to be bored. They want to stay busy; they want to think and make things and explore; they want to have fun and learn! In addition to swimming at the pool or engaging in other outdoor fun, children need to spend some time in mental activity. They need to exercise and develop their minds as well as their bodies. Here are some ways to help your child *progress* rather than *regress* during those long, hot summer days at home:

Encourage your child to engage in *at least one* learning activity daily. On the calendar you can write the name of an activity for each day of the week. Or you can have an "activity bowl" out of which your child draws the name of one activity for each day. These activities combine fun and learning. For example, on the Fourth of July, the child's activity card reads: "See how many words you can make from the letters in INDEPENDENCE." On another day he may be told: "Make a list of major league baseball teams and put them into alphabetical order." You can fill your own "activity bowl" with ideas suitable to your child's age and interests.

A *summer calendar* can keep your child on course while school is not in session. A sample calendar for the month of June follows with suggested activities suitable for preschoolers and early-elementary children. In addition, a blank calendar has been included for your own use. You can fill in the calendar with age-appropriate activities, like some of the ones suggested. You can ask your child's teacher for ideas that would help strengthen the skills he needs to brush up on over the summer. You can check at educational resource stores in your area. (These are not just for teachers; they also stock great source materials for parents and often print a summer learning calendar for their customers.) You can also use any of the other activities mentioned in this book.

Watch the Sunday paper for a Kid's Page, Arts and Crafts Ideas, and Brain Teasers. Clip these throughout the year and keep them on file for summer use. Some magazines also publish a learning idea page or an activity page for children, which you can

			Give your child a list of 10 summer words to put into alphabetical order.
Have your child tape record loud sounds and quiet sounds and then play them for Daddy.	Dinosaur Day! Have your child make a dinosaur out of clay or play dough. Read *Danny and the Dinosaur* by Sid Hoff.	Have your child play hopscotch on your sidewalk.	Give your child play money and grocery ads. He selects money to buy different foods he chooses.
Teach your child a song you learned as a child.	Help your child write a letter to Grandma and Grandpa.	Italian Day: Show your child how to make little meatballs. You add sauce and spaghetti. With a red-checked cloth, have a candlelight dinner.	Have your child name 5 hot things and 5 cold things.
Have your child make a flower arrangement for the dinner table centerpiece.	Library Day: Read a Berenstin Bear book to your child. Kids love them!	Have the child find a bright picture in a magazine, cut it into puzzle shapes, mix up and reassemble them.	Get a piñata. Read about Mexico. Have tacos for dinner.
Have a watermelon seed spitting contest. Let your child have a measuring tape in case it's close.	Take an outing to the fire station. Read your child *Firefighters A to Z* by Jean Johnson.	Talk about our sense of taste. Have your child name some things that taste salty, sweet, sour. Have him taste them.	Go to Farmer's Market in your town or city. Let your child help you pick out produce and make a fruit salad at home.

Library Day: make sure your child has his own library card.	Let your child make real lemonade and invite a friend over.	Play "Simon Says" with your child.
Have your child find as many △ shapes as he can in the house.	Let your child plant flower seeds in the garden or in big tin cans.	Have a cookout at the park and play Frisbee with your child.
Give your child a "Mental Math" problem: $4 + 6 \div 2 \times 5 - 6 = ?$	Have your child make a map of your neighborhood. Mark N, S, E, W directions.	Have your child think of as many animals as he can and make a list of them.
Have your child make a list of *opposites*.	Help your child make paper puppets and put on a puppet show.	Help your child have a spelling bee.
Help your child grow a sweet potato vine in a jar of water.	Give your child pictures of family and friends and let him make an "Album of my Special Friends."	Get out flashcards and review today +, −, ×, ÷ facts (depending on the grade level of your child).

clip and store in your "Summer Learning Ideas" file. Include these in your "activities bowl" or on your summer learning calendar.

Boost Self-Esteem and Build Relationships

In the summer, without the pressure of the school schedule, you have more time to spend and enjoy with your child. Your being positive and giving him encouragement helps build his self-esteem. Learning something new or doing a project together also helps build his confidence in himself, while giving him happy memories of his family and home life. When he returns to school in the fall, he will go back more confident, secure, and able to tackle the new challenges which lie ahead during the school year.

So let summer be a time of building relationships. Don't let your summer schedule become so crowded that you lose out on time spent together with your child. Save time for people in your church and neighborhood also! Invite a family over for dinner and let your child help plan the menu and create the centerpiece. Or have a neighborhood block party and allow your child to make the invitations and help you decorate outdoors. Let each family bring a dish of food, play outdoor games, and enjoy the fellowship of your neighborhood. Spend time with relatives: cousins, aunts, uncles and grandparents.

Spontaneous and Inexpensive Ways to Enjoy Summertime

- Plant and care for a small garden.

- Observe!

  In the daytime, lie out in the grass and watch clouds and their patterns. Ask your child: "What do you see?"

  Sprinkle bread crumbs in the yard, wait quietly nearby and watch the birds.

At night, lie out and watch the stars. Ask: "Do you see the North Star, Big Dipper, Orion?"

- Play in the sprinkler — old-fashioned fun that costs almost nothing and beats the heat.

- "Paint" the sidewalk — with a big paintbrush and a bucket of water!

- Wash dolls, doll clothes and toys with a small pail of water and liquid soap.

- Have a nature scavenger hunt in the backyard. Make a list of things to find: three rocks, a red and yellow flower, four different-shaped leaves, four different-sized sticks, etc., or...

Have a "rainy day" scavenger hunt in the house.

- Experiment with the wind using kites, pinwheels, bright balloons, and bubble-blowing liquid.

- Collect bugs and worms (using a "critter-catcher") and study them under a magnifying glass.

- Have a "Snick-Snacks Cooking Class" for your child (says Candy Snowbarger). Teach him or her to make a snack chosen from a children's cookbook. As you "cook," talk about measurements as the child measures and stirs ingredients. Then the two of you take your snacks, a cool drink and a quilt out into the yard for an impromptu picnic.

Games for Learning

Many games exercise language, memory, visual discrimination and problem-solving skills while the child is having fun and enjoying social interaction. A game as simple as checkers involves planning and problem-solving skills, important for school success. Encourage your child and his friends to turn off the television set in the afternoon hours, stretch out on the floor and play a game.

Although there are many games to choose from, here are a few of the most popular, along with the skills they help improve:

Game	Skill(s) Developed
Memory	Memory and visual discrimination
Hangman	Problem-solving, spelling
Chutes and Ladders	Counting, discrimination
Go to the Head of the Class	Reading and language
Scrabble Alphabet Game	Beginning language and spelling
Scrabble, Scrabble for Juniors	Language, vocabulary building
Monopoly	Planning, problem-solving, math
Tell It Like It Is	Communication, listening
Racko	Math
Connect Four	Planning, problem-solving

Summer Reading Motivation

Teachers advise parents to get a library card for each member of the family and then plan weekly trips to the library to keep their children's reading skills developing. When you take your child to the library each week, don't be in a hurry to leave right away; let him browse among the children's books and periodicals for at least 30 minutes each trip.

A good incentive to keep your child reading during vacation time is the summer reading program provided by most libraries. Incentives range from a coupon for an ice cream cone (awarded for reading 10 books); a sundae, hamburger and French fries (for the next 25 books read); a book bag (for the next 50 books) to many other motivational treats.

You can also set up your own family reading program with similar incentives based on the number of pages read, appropriate for the age of your children. It is helpful to draw up a *reading contract* for each child to sign, in which he agrees in writing to read a certain number of pages each week.

Our friends, the Sargeants, devised a successful summer reading program for their four children. Their youngest son, Ben, was to read 200 pages a week, while Scott, Clayton and Meghan were to read 300 pages weekly. Before any child began reading a selected book, Mom checked to make sure it was on the appropriate reading level. At the end of each week, she tallied the number of pages read by each child. For fulfilling his weekly quota, each child was awarded a trip to an ice cream shop for a sundae; for being on course four weeks he received an all-expense-paid trip to a local pizza parlor which featured video games. For keeping up with his reading schedule all summer long, the industrious child was rewarded with a U.S. savings bond. This incentive program kept all four children reading every spare moment they weren't actually swimming, playing baseball or playing with friends.

Summer Enrichment

Besides all the wonderful summer camps available to youngsters today, most colleges and universities now offer summer enrichment opportunities for children of all ages, including teens. Specialty camps (for interests ranging from computers to sports), art institutes, music festivals, children's drama classes, student stage productions — these and many other programs are offered to encourage the gifts and talents of an enormous variety of young people. Check with your local university for summer enrichment programs offered in your area.

A recent ten-year study revealed that for many families June is one of the most stressful months of the year. For thousands of Americans life is most stressful when children first get out of school and into their parents' hair. How will summer be for *your* family? Boring and frustrating, or exciting and fulfilling? With a little planning, vacation time can be the most enjoyable and satisfying time of the year for your child. He can return to school in the fall rested and refreshed, full of enthusiasm — and ready to *keep* learning!

EPILOGUE

Learning and Unconditional Love

The door opened and my son dragged into the kitchen after losing a tennis match. His downcast eyes reflected feelings of failure. Over a glass of orange juice, he shared his frustrations and disappointment, and I listened.

Finally, before he got up to start his homework, I said with a hug: "I love you regardless. You're special and important to me."

"But I lost," he replied.

"And on other days, you'll have other chances. But I love you."

Those words didn't erase the pain of losing, but I have found that when children come home with a D or F on a test, the disappointment of an athletic failure or the pain of a social crisis that has shaken their world, that is a good opportunity for us as parents to affirm our support for them. When kids are the least successful and lovable, that's the time they need our unconditional love and acceptance the most.

Home should be the place where young people can bring their problems, hurts, and disappointments and be sure of finding understanding, acceptance and security.

> "Do you love me
> Or do you not?
> You told me once
> But I forgot."
>   Anonymous

Too often in our achievement-oriented society, we unknowingly give our children our love and affirmation only when they please us by winning a place on the honor roll or presenting us with a sports victory. We are affectionate when they are being what we want them to be, the ideal son or daughter, the A student, the "star player." By doing so, we subtly deliver the message: "I love you for what you *do and achieve*." Then pressure is put on them to succeed. Pressure to achieve, research shows, leads in fact to *underachievement*, cheating on exams, and the development of low self-esteem.

When they continually fail to measure up to their parents' unrealistic expectations of them, children end up feeling worthless and unlovable.

In contrast, a child who is unconditionally loved, who is encouraged but not pressured, has the courage to step out and risk failure by trying something new in school or work, to ask questions in order to learn.

"The most important factor in the development of children is the quality of love in their family," a counselor said recently. "Children do not learn or mature if they are not loved."

Where does that love come from that causes us to pause in the midst of a wearying day and put aside our own needs in order to love, accept and really "be there" to meet the needs of our child or teenager?

In my experience as a parent, I have come to realize that that kind of love comes only from the God Who loves us with an everlasting love, Who loved us enough to send His own Son to die in our place. And because Christ gave His life for us, we can love others.

As we open our hearts to receive God's love for us as individuals, to heal us of the hurts of our past, and to give us hope for the future, then we are able to give the unconditional love our children so desperately need — a love that doesn't hurry them to be older or smarter or better, but an accepting love for who they are right now. That kind of love is the key that *unlocks* something in a child. It widens a life flow and frees him to change in positive ways, to grow, to learn and to reach his full potential.

Once during a time of concern about our ten-year-old, I found I was becoming critical of his attitudes and actions. I wanted him to change, and he wouldn't. I wanted him to know how much I loved him, and yet irritations pushed us apart.

So I began to pray. The more I prayed for *him,* the more I saw how much *I* needed to change — to accept him just as he was — not just to tolerate, but to actually enjoy and appreciate him! There is a time for correction, but this was a time for acceptance. So I began to pray: "Lord, change *me* inside; help me to be a more loving, patient and understanding mother. Enable me to see my son through Your eyes, not my own."

God began to work in our relationship. He brought love and acceptance where there had been irritation and alienation. Slowly, we began to grow together again.

If any of you lack wisdom, let him ask of God, that giveth to all men liberally, and upbraideth not; and it shall be given him (James 1:5). As we pray, God gives us wisdom about how to teach, correct and guide our children, how to channel their boundless energy. He gives us the extra love and patience we need.

Parenting is an enormous job requiring almost limitless reserves of inner strength. To be decisive, to set family guidelines and then stick by them; to listen attentively and patiently at the end of a tiring, frustrating day; to always *"be there"* when we are

191

needed — all this demands great emotional, physical, and spiritual resources. We are needed, and we often feel so inadequate for the task.

But I have found that in our relationship with Jesus Christ, in His Word and in prayer, God has provided us tremendous resources. He gives us the unconditional love our children so desperately need to flourish and bloom — not just when they succeed, but also in the midst of soccer defeats, failing test grades, and spilled milk.

As the mother of John and Charles, Susanna Wesley was a woman of unusual strength and unequalled devotion. Her biography describes how she used to tuck her children in bed each night. As she lifted her candle to gaze upon each face, she prayed that God would enable her to so inspire her children that they could one day be used by Him to change the world.

An electric light makes no difference in a dark room until it is turned on. But once brought into contact with the source of power, it provides illumination. We are like that light. Connected to the Divine Power Source, as we commit ourselves and our children daily to God, we become channels of His love and guidance — channels for His light and truth to flow to our children so their lives will some day shine before men in such a way that they will see their good works, and glorify their Father Who is in heaven. (Matt. 5:16.)

Let us continue in the adventure of preparing for life these precious children who are with us for such a short time — walking hand in hand with the One Who loves them even more than we do!

BIBLIOGRAPHY

Beecher, Henry Ward. *Proverbs from Plymouth Pulpit.* 1887.

Dobson, James. *Hide or Seek: Self-Esteem for the Child.* Old Tappan: Fleming H. Revell Company, 1974.

Campbell, Ross. *How to Really Love Your Child.* New York: Signet Books, 1982.

Dunn, Rita. "Learning Styles: Link Between Individual Differences Effective Instruction." *North Carolina Educational Leadership,* 1986.

"Family Problems: How They're Affecting Today's Classrooms." *Learning 86,* Vol. 14, No. 5. Jan. 1986.

Gardner, Howard. *Frames of Mind: The Theory of Multiple Intelligences.* New York: Basic Books, Inc., 1983.

Garlett, Marti. *Who Will Be My Teacher?* Waco: Word Books, 1985.

Golick, Margie. *Deal Me In: The Use of Playing Cards in Teaching and Learning.* New York: Monarch Press, Simon and Schuster, Inc., 1985.

Graves, Robert and Stuart, Virginia. *Write From the Start: Tapping Your Child's Natural Writing Ability.* New York: E.P. Dutton, 1985.

Homework: Helping Students Achieve. American Association of School Administrators. Arlington, Virginia, 1985.

Kelsey, Morton. *CARING: How Can We Love One Another?* New York: Paulist Press, 1981.

Meigs, Cornelia. *Invincible Louisa.* New York: Little, Brown and Company, 1933.

"Memorization: Making It Work in Your Class." *Learning,* Nov.-Dec. 1985.

Newsweek, Feb. 11, 1980.

Prevention, June 1985.

Sawtelle, Charlotte. *Learning Is a Family Affair.* Maine Department of Educational and Cultural Services, 1984.

Science Digest, Oct., 1983.

Shaeffer, Edith. *What Is a Family?* Old Tappan: Fleming H. Revell Company, 1975.

Schimmels, Cliff. *How to Help Your Child Survive and Thrive in Public School.* Old Tappan: Fleming H. Revell Company, 1982.

Smith, Frank. *Essays into Literacy.* Portsmouth: Heinemann Educational Books, 1983.

Trelease, Jim. *The Read-Aloud Handbook.* New York: Viking Penguin Inc., 1986.

What Works: Research About Teaching and Learning. United States Department of Education. William J. Bennett, Secretary, 1986.

Winn, Marie. *Unplugging the Plug-In Drug: Help Your Children Kick the TV Habit.* New York: Viking Press, 1987.

"Writing Report Card." National Assessment of Educational Progress Report, Princeton, NJ, 1986.

"Your Home Is Your Child's First School." International Reading Association, Newark, DE.

Zaslavsky, Claudia. *Preparing Young Children for Math: A Book of Games.* New York: Schocken Books, 1979.